Beyond Decline

BEYOND DECLINE

A challenge to the churches

Robin Gill

SCM PRESS LTD

Copyright © Robin Gill 1988

British Library Cataloguing in Publication Data

Gill, Robin
  Beyond decline: a challenge to the
  churches.
  1. Society. Role of Christian church
  I. Title
  261.1

  ISBN 0–334–00097–1

First published 1988 by
SCM Press Ltd
26–30 Tottenham Road London N1 4BZ

Printed in Great Britain by
Billing and Sons Ltd, Worcester

Contents

Introduction

Perhaps the most obvious thing one can say about the churches in
Britain today is that they are declining. Churchgoers themselves are
well aware of this as are sociologists of religion. The facts are
evident. Congregations in most churches are far smaller than they
were even twenty years ago and the churchgoing public is now less
than a sixth of its size at the height of Victorian churchgoing. The
number of clergy is declining, the proportion of clergy to the
general population is declining, the number of church buildings is
declining, Sunday schools are declining, communicants are declining, even at Easter and Christmas, baptisms and confirmations are
declining. The list is long and depressing. It has been mapped out
expertly in books such as Robert Currie, Alan Gilbert and Lee
Horsley's *Churches and Churchgoers*[1] and needs no further mapping
out here.

Decline is a fact and is accepted as such here. However, responses to decline vary considerably. This book has been written to
challenge some of these responses.

I have deliberately written this book both as an academic and as
an active parish priest. As an academic my training has been in both
theology and sociology and I will attempt to use these two disci-
plines here. It is important to be able to analyse as coolly as possible
the various responses to decline that are evident within the churches.
However, I believe that it is important to treat these responses
theologically as well. It will soon become clear that my understanding of theology intimately involves my experience as a parish priest.
I suppose that it might have been possible to write about responses
to church decline from a purely academic perspective. Yet for me
this would have been most undesirable. My various worlds so

patently meet at this point. Responses to church decline are certainly interesting sociologically. Theologically they can be somewhat depressing. Pastorally they are of central concern. Indeed the last demands some knowledge of the other two.

In the first chapter I examine the way decline has led to what I believe is a disastrous anti-intellectualism within the British churches. As an academic and as a priest I find this distrust of critical theology extremely worrying. For me it is symptomatic of an increasing gulf between theory and practice. It is a gulf that is the very reverse of some of the most exciting developments in recent theology.

In the second chapter I examine ways in which declining churches are tempted to compensate by pressing for general assemblies and synods to make specific moral and social pronouncements. It is very tempting to believe that declining churches in a pluralist society should become lobby groups for particular causes. If churches are no longer central to the aims of society they can at least seek to change specific practices within society. They can compensate for marginalization by offering members of society a distinctive perspective on a range of moral and social issues. In arguing against this approach I am aware that I am contesting activities that still dominate general assemblies and synods.

In the third chapter I will set out five alternative options for Christians to engage in moral and social issues. They are not mutually compatible. Indeed they are meant to show some of the real choices that Christians must make if they are to change society. I am convinced that Christians should seek to change society, but I am also convinced that we should be far more clear-headed about how we might actually do this. If we are to avoid the temptations of decline – either to be too specific as churches or quite oppositely to eschew moral and social issues altogether – we must become more seriously aware of the effective options for social change.

Another temptation posed by decline concerns evangelism. In the fourth chapter I will examine various models of evangelism and church growth. Again I will be critical. I am not at all convinced by radicals who disdain any concept of church growth. For me it is essential that churches attempt to reach as deeply as possible into the community. And that includes attempting to draw as many as possible into their own worship. Nevertheless, I will argue that some dominant models of evangelism are far too simplistic and contribute to the anti-intellectualism apparent within the churches. As society becomes better educated simplistic evangelism cannot be an adequate response to decline. Instead I will set out an alternative model for parish life, organization and worship.

The fifth chapter will examine parish structures and clergy deployment within the declining churches. From my own experience of fifteen years of non-stipendiary parish ministry, as priest-in-charge of an urban, a rural and now a small town parish, I am convinced that churches are not deploying clergy in the most effective way to counter decline. Again there is an acute gap between theory and practice. Churches increasingly claim that they are concerned with the needs of the inner city. Yet in practice they spend a quite disproportionate amount of resources on the countryside. I will suggest a radical model for deployment which might even edge the churches beyond decline.

In the final chapter I will return to the theme of faith. I will try to unpack the implications of my understanding of faith as a relationship – our common relationship to God in Christ. Its implications for ecumenism are particularly important. It also contrasts sharply with the reductionist responses to secularism and decline of theologians such as Don Cupitt.

My aim is to challenge but also to be positive. It is too easy to produce negative critiques of institutional churches. It is much harder, but in the end more important, to suggest workable alternatives. I am convinced that churches with vision and courage could change. Having just finished *Theology and Sociology: a Reader*,[2] I fully intended to continue with my long-term project – an account of theology as a social system.[3] However there was too much happening in the British churches which I felt needed to be challenged. And my own ministry unearthed questions which simply would not go away. It also served to clarify for me a positive alternative for the churches.

A number of people have read or heard earlier drafts of this book. Some forty ordinands on the North East and Carlisle Ordination Courses heard the contents at their summer conferences and provided many valuable corrections. Professor Duncan Forrester of Edinburgh University once again offered many detailed and extremely helpful criticisms. His Centre for Theology and Public Issues continues to be a major stimulus and challenge to the churches. Dr John Bowden, Managing Director of SCM Press, has been most encouraging and generous in sharing insights from his own twenty years of non-stipendiary ministry. Bishop Richard Holloway of the Diocese of Edinburgh has been extremely helpful, despite his many commitments, in reading a later draft. Finally my love and thanks to Jenny for reading the fifth chapter, even though she has heard many of its ideas over the last twenty years.

1

Decline and the Gulf between Theory and Practice

Academic theology is increasingly viewed with suspicion within the declining British churches and particularly by the clergy who are confronted most directly with this decline. Theologians are frequently regarded as out of touch with the realities of church life and their views are regarded with considerable suspicion. At a time of radical financial cuts within the universities, faculties and departments of theology have received little help, support, or even encouragement from the churches. And there are many who appear to believe that academic theologians serve only to confuse and bewilder the faithful and even contribute directly to church decline.

Curiously, most academic theologians in Britain are still church members. In many faculties and departments of theology (including my own) the overwhelming majority of academics give freely of their time to various churches both at national and at parish levels. Nonetheless I think it is also possible to detect a growing impatience at the anti-intellectualism so often expressed within the churches. And there is a fear that declining churches are becoming less and less intelligent just at the very moment that academic standards are rising in society at large.

I believe that this gulf is disastrous for the churches and unjust to academic theologians. It will be a constant theme of this book that theory and practice must go together. Of course it is perfectly possible to have a system of academic theology which has little concern for church membership. There are some very fine secular theologians, especially in the United States where the gulf is far wider. And of course academic knowledge is not and never has been a prerequisite for being a Christian. There are many saints who would not have satisfied university entrance requirements! Yet churches which refuse to apply critical intelligence to themselves and which, in response to decline, marginalize their own academic theologians, must expect to occupy a less than central role in an educated and thinking society. Practice which is untested by critical theory soon becomes blind. Even if the latter is uncomfortable and disturbing, reflective practice cannot afford to ignore it.

There is a growing recognition by those academic theologians who have taken political theology and especially liberation theology seriously that theory and practice are intimately related.[1] Sometimes the Greek word 'praxis' is used to denote an understanding of Christian practice which is seriously related to theory. Whereas the term 'practice' simply refers to any form of observable action, the term 'praxis' is reserved for those forms of action which flow from and contribute directly to theory. Such an understanding of 'praxis' maintains that Christian beliefs necessarily involve Christian action and that this action moulds one's understanding of the beliefs. 'Praxis' implies that critical reflection is not some optional extra which can be left to those who teach academic theology. But it also implies that those who do teach academic theology should themselves be involved in the action. It is precisely this understanding which is central to my own work and which contributes to my present unease.

Given this understanding of the relation between theory and practice it is hardly surprising that I do see a serious link between my work as an academic and my work as a parish priest. At first they appear to be rather distinct. The academic work is done in the setting of a large university faculty with an exceedingly strong intellectual tradition. Further, this job requires me to have separate postgraduate degrees in theology and sociology. My parish work, in contrast, takes place some miles away in the Scottish Borders (where my wife is a GP). The ecumenism which is simply taken for granted in the faculty, with Roman Catholics, Presbyterians, Anglicans and many other denominations regularly sharing the eucharist together, is light years away from ecumenism in the Borders. The degree of doctrinal openness which is now an essential feature of an ecumenical faculty is still regarded by many in the Borders as dangerous and threatening. Political causes on issues such as South Africa or nuclear deterrence which are second nature to students in the faculty are viewed quite differently by many in the Borders.

And biblical criticism which is resisted by some students but accepted by most remains foreign territory to many in the Borders. These do seem to be two quite distinct worlds and my role in each undoubtedly differs.

Yet there are links between them and for me these are quite crucial. Many of the students in the faculty are training for ordained ministry or are already ordained ministers, albeit in some fifteen different denominations. In Scotland I am delighted to be able to say that this also includes many of the women students. Slowly they learn that I too am still a parish priest. I certainly do not see my role as trying to impart hints and tips to them on how they should become 'good ministers'. That understanding of practical or pastoral theology has been extinct at Edinburgh for some twenty years. It was always a flawed model which tended to gain scant respect from students and which ignored the obvious point that serious professional training takes place best not in lecture rooms but in supervised pastoral placements. Rather it gives the students and myself a common basis of current involvement in parish ministry. We are aware of the same problems and potentialities. We share a common concern to face them seriously. And, perhaps most important of all, neither they nor I regard parish ministry as second-best. They know that I did not become an academic to escape parish ministry.

The links from the academic world to the parish are even stronger. I seriously believe that I do not teach one thing to the students and another to the congregation. I believe that congregations are fully capable of thought and of critical growth. Over a period of twelve years with the same country congregation I found that it was more than possible to introduce critical ideas, to raise moral and social issues, to treat the Bible critically yet constructively, and to develop a greater awareness of ecumenism. It is for others to judge how successful I was in actually achieving any of these objectives. That is not my point. My point is that I did not feel any deep dichotomy in the teaching I was doing in the two quite different contexts. Of course the form was different. It would be nonsense to use the technical terms that would be appropriate for university students on a country congregation. But then every teacher is aware of adapting language in differing contexts, even within the differing contexts presented by first and final year students. Again any teacher is aware of differences of intelligence in an audience. For some students sequential ideas have to be taken slowly with plenty of helpful illustrations, whereas for others illustrations serve only to irritate. Ideas may have to move more slowly in most (but certainly not in all) congregations than they might for students. Yet they can still be the same ideas. And both groups are capable of growth and change.

However, for me the strength of the parish link is not simply in the challenge of interpreting ideas in two different contexts but in actually testing out these ideas. Again this is praxis rather than just practice. In terms of praxis the validity of theological notions is actually put to the test in the context of a worshipping community. Theological notions and models are not just of interest as intellectual notions and models, they are of central concern as moulders of and responders to action. The context provided by a congregation becomes a very serious testing ground for theology. If an idea can be communicated without the assistance of technical jargon, can be used coherently within a congregation that is prepared to correct an erring preacher, can be discussed in a house-group and can be developed over a period of years with the same community, it can in the process be tested more adequately than elsewhere. The university certainly provides one sort of testing ground, but the parish is in many respects a far more demanding testing ground. On many occasions I have been grateful to the congregation for providing this.

If the link then is seen in the first place as being from the university to the parish it eventually transpires that the most crucial link goes back from the parish to the university. Of course the parish also supplies numerous sociological insights which contribute to the other side of my academic work. Yet I regard the specifically theological contribution as the more important. Praxis theology needs to be sustained by deep roots in the Christian community.

Theology also needs to take into account the realities of church life. One of the sharpest functions of sociology is to measure intentions and strategies against attainments and practices. Much of my academic work has been concerned with trying to relate what is said theoretically by theologians on issues such as war or abortion to their social contexts, constraints and intended or unintended consequences.[2] Theologians have not usually been very good at doing this. Churches too have a tendency to romanticize features of their life and to ignore the realities of the finite and sometimes sinful communities which really constitute them.

This point was made very effectively by Paul Badham of Lampeter University in a recent critique of the Lima report. Badham recognizes, as a committed priest himself, the ecumenical importance of the report *Baptism, Eucharist and Ministry*. He believes that it is significant that over one hundred church theologians from such a wide variety of traditions felt that they could recommend their report to their own churches on issues that had so divided them in the past. Yet what worries Badham is the gap between what is claimed about the church life in relation to these three topics and the reality that the empirical churches present. His most telling arguments come in the first part of his article and concern baptism.

He starts by setting out the New Testament claims about baptism that are contained in the Lima report. Here baptism is 'the sign of new life through Jesus Christ'; it is 'participation in Christ's death and resurrection'; it is a washing away of sin; it is a new birth; an enlightenment by Christ; the experience of salvation from the flood; an exodus from bondage; it is a liberation into a new humanity in which barriers of division, whether of sex, race, or social class, are transcended.

Badham then argues pointedly as follows:

> This passage is a sustained catena of New Testament quotations but how are these quotations to be understood? If we interpret them as laying down what baptism *should be*, then clearly they are very significant. We could readily agree that participation in the Christian community *should* help us to be enlightened by Christ, should lead to a new ethical orientation, and *should* lead to a new experience of humanity in which barriers of sex, race and social class are transcended. But it must be acknowledged that the churches as they are at present fall so far short of these ideals, that a complete transformation of their ethos would be required before one could begin to see any approximation between these ideals and the empirical situation in the contemporary church.[3]

Here lies Badham's problem. The sociological evidence which he proceeds to cite all points to empirical churches which are not characterized by the kind of new humanity in which the barriers of sex, race and social class have been broken down at all.[4] Indeed, the strongest evidence suggests that, particularly in the United

States,[5] but even in Britain[6] as well, there is a connection between racism and church membership. So he argues that 'in country after country the identification between the Christian church and the national heritage militates strongly against any claim that the church constitutes a new humanity which is free from any racial or national identification'.[7]

The sociological evidence that Badham cites here needs to be handled carefully. It would be too bold to claim that there is a direct causal link established between racism and Christianity. Rather there is a fairly consistent correlation between nominal forms of churchgoing and racism and an even stronger correlation between nominal churchgoing and anti-semitism. There is also a correlation between some fundamentalist forms of Christian belief and anti-semitism. When this correlation is set alongside historical evidence, especially about Christian attitudes towards Jews, there are strong grounds for suspecting that the churches' record in this area is not good.[8] Some Christians have been deeply implicated in racism and many have done little to oppose it. If this is expressed in the positive terms of Christianity bringing about a new humanity in which racism is overcome then Badham's point is surely made. At an empirical level it would seem that historical Christianity is a part of the problem of racism, and particularly of anti-semitism.

On social class Badham is again able to point to well-established sociological evidence. In survey after survey of religious belonging and belief, social class (however measured) is a major feature.[9] British churches are overwhelmingly middle-class institutions. This is especially true of national churches such as the Church of England and the Church of Scotland, but it is even true, albeit to a less extent, of Roman Catholicism and the smaller denominations. And even on sexual barriers Badham cites David Martin's verdict that churches are 'a central bastion of male supremacy': 'and one cannot read collections of essays against the ordination of women without becoming aware of how deep-rooted an antipathy towards women lies behind many of the arguments presented'.[10]

The way is now prepared for Badham's conclusion:

> The record of the churches on issues of race, sex and class would not normally affect a discussion of the meaning of baptism. When all the churches apparently agree at Lima that *the meaning* of baptism is that through it we are liberated into a new kind of

humanity in which divisions of sex, race and class are transcended, one has to ask what meaning can be attached to such
words when they so contradict the reality of the church's life.[11]

I have presented this argument in detail because it is so unusual
coming from a theologian. Sociologists of religion regard such
evidence as commonplace and Christian ethicists are beginning to
take more note of empirical evidence and to temper some of their
claims about the churches. But theologians in general, and those
representing their churches in particular, have been remarkably
oblivious to the obvious discrepancy highlighted by Badham. If
there is a growing gulf appearing between academic theologians
and the clergy, then there is also a gulf between the claims of
church theologians about their churches and the empirical realities
to which they refer. Sociology can play quite an effective role in
pin-pointing this gulf. Naturally it is important to make it clear that
sociology is not simply taking over the role of theology. An empirical description of churches, as they are, ought never to be confused
with a prescriptive theological vision of the church, as it should be.
Badham is fully aware of this distinction. His point is rather that the
gulf between the two is at present uncomfortably wide.

The uncomfortable position I will take in this book is that
churches should be much more rigorous than at present in relating
theory and practice. It is far too comfortable to select brands of
theology which reinforce an idealized picture of the churches. It is
distinctly less comfortable to work with a theology which acknow-
ledges the ambiguities of church life. It is too comfortable to pro-
nounce on doctrinal, moral or social issues as if particular churches,
despite their numerical decline, have united theories and practices.
It is much more uncomfortable to work seriously with the observation that churches are pluralistic institutions containing competing
claims of authority and interpretation.

Precisely because many university faculties and departments of
theology have become increasingly ecumenical they have been
forced to confront this pluralism and ambiguity. If once it might
have been possible for Anglican faculties in England and Presbyterian faculties in Scotland to have been relatively inured against
this pluralism, today it is not. Over the last two decades there has
been a radical transformation of the ecclesiastical construction of
most faculties and departments. There are still a number of chairs

with a strong, and sometimes wholly rigid, bias towards Anglicanism in England or Presbyterianism in Scotland. Hopefully this too will go. However in terms of faculty membership as a whole the situation has changed radically. Most, but certainly not all, academic theologians are practising Christians. Yet the ethos is no longer restricted to particular denominations. Indeed there is a sharp reaction against theologians who still work as if other Christian traditions did not exist or could simply be marginalized.

This change of ethos is immediately evident if one compares the syllabus of a faculty now and that of the same faculty twenty years ago. Twenty years ago when I finished studying at London University it was still assumed that basic doctrine could finish at Chalcedon. The Reformation was treated as an optional extra and ethics was a new discipline freshly added to the syllabus. Eastern Christianity and Third World Christianity scarcely featured, if at all. Even biblical scholarship, which was certainly much influenced by reformed, continental, biblical criticism, seldom considered that there was much to be learned outside North America and Europe. When I first came to Edinburgh fifteen years ago the syllabus had begun to change. Ethics had always been more important in the Presbyterian tradition and naturally a study of the Reformation was considered essential. But there were still some other rather curious gaps. It was considered legitimate to study ethics using primary texts from Luther and Calvin but not Aquinas. Natural law could be treated (and rejected) in one or possibly two lectures. And, like London, it was North America and Europe which dictated the agenda in both theology and biblical studies.

Today the situation has changed and is still changing. There are now far greater similarities between the expectations of London and Edinburgh. Both have become seriously ecumenical in their staff, with Roman Catholics playing an increasing role in the mainstream of theological life. Both expect students to read deeply in a range of theological traditions, including non-Western forms of liberation theology. Both include a study of some of the most important social criticisms of Christianity – Marx, Durkheim, Freud, etc. – as a part of the basic syllabus. In both students are drawn from a very wide variety of Christian traditions. In short, Christian pluralism is a fact of daily life in a university in a form which is less apparent at first sight in theological seminaries and within particular denominations.

However, even this difference is beginning to disappear. Theological seminaries are taught by theologians who have been trained in universities and their students can read for themselves academic non-denominational theology. Even the syllabus and library resources of highly conservative Bible colleges have begun to reflect this change. Pluralism is a fact of life in theological training in Britain today. Slowly it will begin to filter into congregations too. Of course in a real sense it is already there. Anyone who has conducted an open discussion on doctrinal, moral or social issues within a house-group will be fully aware that there are enormous differences of opinion and even practice amongst ordinary church members. The predominant expectation of congregations and clergy alike may still be that congregations *should* be united, at least on doctrinal issues. But the reality is very different. Once again there is a very obvious discrepancy between theory and practice.

This particular discrepancy can be found at many levels of church life. It has been a persistent feature of inter-church conversations. The predominant expectation has been that individual churches involved in such conversations should first set out their own doctrinal positions. Then they should note the differences that exist between their own positions and those of the other churches involved in the conversation. Finally the various churches together should work towards a united statement of belief. This process is so well established that it is difficult to see that it is founded upon faulty premises. It presumes that individual churches do in fact have, or at least ought to have, unified patterns of belief. Doctrinal pluralism, which in reality characterizes most denominations, is presumably viewed in this process as an error which must be overcome. I shall return to this point in the final chapter.

Much of this book is going to be spent observing and criticizing the way declining churches make this presumption of uniformity. It can be found in their attempts to arrive at united positions on a range of moral and social issues. It is also evident in prominant understandings of mission and outreach. And it has been a persistent feature in recent doctrinal debates and controversies. In each of these areas there is a clear discrepancy between theory and practice. A level of uniformity is presumed and sought which bears little relationship to the empirical reality of present-day Christianity. Further, it is a type of uniformity more suitable to an age which studied theology in numerically strong denominational enclaves than to the present era of university theology. Ironically the very type of uniformity which is open to churches – a careful ordering and deployment of ministry to meet the needs of an urban industrial society – is a uniformity sometimes sought in theory but habitually resisted in practice.

One of the most striking recent examples of a declining church seeking an elusive doctrinal uniformity revolves around the Bishop of Durham's publicly expressed doubts about the corporality of the virgin birth and resurrection. The example is all the more important because it also illustrates the growing gulf between academic theology and the churches. One of the most frequent responses by clergy to David Jenkins' television appearance shortly before becoming Bishop of Durham was that he should learn to distinguish between what is appropriate for university students and what is appropriate for Christians generally. It was maintained repeatedly that, although academic theologians had been arguing about the corporality of the virgin birth and the resurrection for most of this century, such a debate would only confuse and disturb the remaining faithful. Some argued more forcefully than this. For them, someone who expressed such doubts had no business to be made a bishop or perhaps even to remain a priest. Both groups clearly believed there to be a gulf between university and church and even the moderate group considered that David Jenkins had acted incautiously, inappropriately, and in a manner likely to contribute further to the decline of the Church of England.

As a priest in the Newcastle diocese at the time it was difficult to avoid the waves stirred up by the controversy. However I soon discovered a difference which I had not expected. With my own congregation, in which I had been preaching for ten years, I encountered little problem in talking freely about the issues of faith involved. Together we were well aware that Christians do have internal disagreements about such doctrinal issues. Indeed when I preached directly on the corporality of the resurrection on Easter Sunday, expressing difficulties with some of the traditional arguments about the empty tomb and directly referring to David Jenkins, much discussion was generated. Most of the congregation seemed well able to distinguish between an understanding of the resurrection which generally united us and the issue of corporality which did not. Those on the conservative doctrinal side naturally wished me to be more fulsome in their support. Whereas those who were more radical teased me about sitting on the fence! Yet both groups were fully aware that the issue had caused disagreement amongst Christians for many years. I searched hard to find the faithful who were supposed to be so confused and disturbed.

Unfortunately I found them a few weeks later. I was asked to preach in a neighbouring church while the priest was away. I preached what I thought was an eirenic sermon on faith. I expressed the view that faith is primarily about a relationship – our relationship to God in Christ – rather than about propositions. The congregation seemed to be responsive until I referred in passing to the Bishop of Durham. Nothing was said at the time, but within two weeks a petition had been organized in the congregation against the Bishop of Durham and I was discreetly informed that I would not be invited back to preach. I am sure that the fault was mine. After ten years with the same congregation, I had forgotten about the expectations of a more traditional congregation. Obviously I had not sufficiently prepared the ground. The congregation still expected uniformity of belief from Christians, despite the fact that to my knowledge individuals within that very congregation expressed their faith very differently from each other.

I suspect that our perceptions of the local controversy were quite different. They doubtless saw me as a typical academic. As an academic I would inevitably defend another academic, David Jenkins. As an academic I was out of touch with what ordinary folk believe and as an academic I was party to a dangerous and damaging world of theological speculation. Despite my ministry in the neighbouring church and despite mutual friends and supporting parishioners, I still represented a threatening academic world. My perception was inevitably somewhat different. I saw a good, faithful and friendly congregation in a very beautiful little country church expecting a level of doctrinal uniformity which they themselves did not share. Far from the issues being simply generated by academic theologians I saw a diversity of Christian beliefs about resurrection within the congregation which was if anything actually wider than those currently held within the academic world. Ironically the views of theologians tend to cluster around a limited number of options. They learn to distinguish between the sort of Greek Platonism that is often apparent within congregations and the more specifically Judaeo-Christian assumptions about resurrection which characterize the New Testament. As a result they seldom espouse today theories about the transmigration of the soul, about fate, about astrology, or about reincarnation. Yet I have discovered all of these beliefs amongst local church-goers.

I suspect that our small local controversy mirrored the Jenkins controversy at a national level. One group observed a gulf between academic theologians and the churches. The other group observed a gulf between what Christians often say that they believe and what they actually believe. I am sure that both gulfs are equally unnecessary and that both need to be bridged. The issues debated by theologians today are not usually so divorced from the active life of the church. They can certainly be corrected by this and should, as I have argued, regard church life as an important test of theological validity. In turn, I am convinced that congregations can be led gently towards a more discerning and critical understanding of Christian beliefs. Indeed, a genuine path to Christian unity may not be discovered until Christians generally are more prepared to discern and appreciate the pluralism of Christianity in its many forms. The gospel is too rich to be captured in single forms. Once Christian faith is seen primarily as a relationship – our relationship to God in Christ – Christians may learn not to confuse partial doctrines and forms of words with the relationship itself.

The House of Bishops' statement on the issues to the General Synod of the Church of England unfortunately contains within it both understandings of Christian faith. At one level *The Nature of Christian Belief* is an attempt to combine a variety of understandings of the nature of beliefs about the virgin birth and resurrection. It is scarcely surprising that the bishops themselves are not united on the issue of the corporality of the virgin birth and resurrection. At one point they say that 'faith is a personal response; and it responds most naturally to the kind of affirmation which itself springs from a personal relationship'![12] They even insist that 'the questioning and creative process is a necessary part of Christian discipleship' and that 'in the past, crucial insights have been won by those who had the courage to question in faith. The Church of England is committed to this process with openness and integrity, and with a confidence, born of experience, that, however exacting it may be, essential truths of the Gospel will emerge from it more clearly understood, and better able to bring help and illumination to a world caught in the confusion of ever more rapid change'.[13] The tone of the statement as whole is eirenic and deliberately inclusive. So whilst the majority clearly believes that corporality properly 'expresses the faith of the Church of England', the statement is careful not to make negative remarks about the status of those who do not accept corporality. Some [14] immediately attacked the statement for lack of precision on this point, but it is clear that it is intentional and deliberately inclusive.

Other parts of the statement, however, seem to see faith as assent to uniform propositions. So, at one point, the bishops argue as follows:

> The truth or otherwise of the claim that Jesus was conceived by a divine creative act without a human father is, in any case, something that could never be settled by any testimony human beings could supply. In that respect it needs to be recognized that a critical weighing of New Testament indications is bound to be an inconclusive and even marginal exercise. In the end the decision has to be a matter of faith.[15]

The term faith is so often used in this second sense that its oddity is not at once apparent. Involved is almost a popular understanding of faith as something you decide to accept without any real evidence. Unfortunately it fits uneasily alongside the relational understanding of faith just cited. Christian churches could conceivably require members to believe things on trust and with only ambiguous evidence. They have indeed done just that at times in the past. But it is hardly a very elevating or intelligent understanding of faith. And, when faith is seen in relational terms, it is difficult to see to what present-day 'responses' to God in Christ doctrines of corporality are meant to refer the believer. Unfortunately the bishops show that they are aware that the New Testament evidence about the corporality of either the virgin birth or the resurrection is found in some sources and not others. So they seem to be tempted to supplement the evidence with propositional faith.

They are also tempted to use arguments which illustrate rather forcefully the growing gulf between academic theology and the churches. The following paragraph is worth quoting in full:

> On the assumption that the Empty Tomb was part of the earliest Easter preaching, another important consideration comes into play. If opponents of Jesus had removed the body, then when the Easter message was first proclaimed they had decisive evidence

with which to discredit it. Why did they not do so? If Jesus's followers were responsible it has to be assumed not only that they were lying, but that they were able to lie with such conviction as to convert thousands, and, more unbelievably still, that they were prepared to suffer and die joyfully for their fabrication. Against such a hypothesis of fraud or religious psychosis the whole ethic and character of the New Testament are a sufficient and eloquent witness.[16]

An argument such as this, which bypasses redaction and herme- neutical scholarship would, I am afraid, receive very few marks even for a first year university student. The Gospels are suddenly treated as contemporary accounts which could be disputed by immediate witnesses. They are presented as if we have access to the views of *any* contemporary critics. And then, to make matters worse, the whole is presented in a simplistic bad-mad-or-true type argument. Even some of my teenage parishioners were able to spot the obvious flaw in this argument: people, especially those who already have strong convictions, can quite simply be mistaken. *Ex post facto* rationalization is hardly an unknown phenomenon and anyone who has listened to sincere Mormons defending their accounts of the rise of Mormonism will be well aware that religious people do at times adopt some unusual historical perspectives.

The arguments that the bishops finally use to convince others of the corporality of the virgin birth are distinctly more sophisticated. Unfortunately the drift of their prior argument has constructed a fairly powerful thesis to the effect that only certain parts of the New Testament seem to be aware of the doctrine and that it might be questioned 'whether any human being created by such a divine act could be authentically one with us in our full humanity, and ... that if he is not then it is the Church's central belief in the Incarnation which has been destroyed'.[17]

They then argue as follows:

Nevertheless, there are also questions to be asked about the claim that an authentic humanity can exist only as a result of normal human procreation. First, if it is the eternally existent Second Person of the Blessed Trinity who is also the one person of the Incarnate Lord Jesus Christ, then would it not follow that this human act of procreation must have been frustrated by God from achieving its normal result, namely the genesis of a new

human person. Secondly, without endorsing any of the older
theories which linked human sinfulness with sexual generation,
would not the child of human parents inevitably share our imper-
fect human nature. And are there not difficulties in the belief
that God was able to live out his essential character of holy love
in such a nature? It can fairly be argued that this view of Jesus's
human origins calls for special divine intervention quite as radical as in the traditional account of the Virginal Conception.[18]

It is difficult to see that the full weight of their thesis about the
corporality of the virgin birth can rest upon these two arguments.
The first is framed more in the language and terms of Chalcedon
than the New Testament and mixes the concept of personhood in
this with what is presumably a reference to a present-day concept
of 'a new human person'. And the second comes very close to
suggesting that Jesus was not a full human being at all. In an
academic context such arguments would need considerable un-
packing if they were to be acceptable. Presented as an offering to
the church at large they are cryptic and unconvincing.

My point in citing these arguments from *The Nature of Christian
Belief* is not to engage in the theological issues at this stage. Rather
it is to illustrate the present gap between academic theology and the
churches. Some of the bishops who produced the statement are
certainly familiar with present-day academic theology, but others
are clearly not. This in part may account for some of the uneven-
ness noted in the document. It is not a polemical or an exclusive
work and it does show some real understanding of the role of
theological enquiry. Nonetheless it does have some naive and un-
critical moments. Most worrying of all, it in part reinforces the
conviction that fully critical enquiry should be reserved for academics. The faithful need reassurance.

From my own ministry I believe that this conviction is mistaken.
Even when the faithful claim that they need reassurance, there are
grounds for holding that they are capable of accepting doctrinal
differences of opinion. If they were to look more closely at themselves, they could realize that doctrinal differences already exist
amongst the faithful. Further, they might be led to see that an
increasingly educated society needs a more, rather than less, intelligent and critical approach to doctrine, from bishops as well.

2

The Gulf in Social Pronouncements

Most church assemblies and synods today feel the need to make pronouncements upon a range of moral and social issues. Even though they are fully aware that their role in society is more marginal than it might have been before their current state of decline, they still feel this need. Some commentators have even contended that this felt need is actually a symptom of decline. As churches decline and become more marginal in a pluralist society so they seek to compensate by taking specific positions on moral and social issues. In effect they become like other lobby groups in society. Thus it becomes important that 'The Church of England', 'The Methodist Church', 'The Church of Scotland', etc. should have a position on the central moral and social issues which confront British society today. In democratic churches a great deal of work and discussion goes into producing reports on such issues and in trying to have them adopted by their general assemblies or synods. It is felt to be important that churches should be seen to be actively engaged in deliberating specific moral and social issues, in seeking to mould public opinion on them and, if necessary seeking to alter legislation. Sometimes this task is identified as the prophetic role of the churches which will restore their credibility despite their current decline. It seems so obvious to many both within and outside the churches that churches as churches should have such a role in society, that it may seem foolish to question it.

It may also be dangerous to question it. Those who do so are usually assumed to be traditionalists who believe that 'churches should keep out of politics'. They are assumed to belong to that group which maintains that the public role of the churches is to attend to the specifically 'religious' needs of society, eschewing all matters which properly concern politicians. Edward Norman has sometimes appeared to support such a position, arguing that the politicization of the churches actually contributes to their decline.[1] It is not just a symptom but a prime contributant. On this understanding public policy on nuclear deterrence, sanctions against South Africa, unemployment, urban deprivation, the Stock Exchange, and perhaps even abortion and pornography, is of concern to politicians and the electorate rather than to churches. The word 'perhaps' is important in this sentence. There are indications to suggest that matters of family and sexual morality are usually excluded by traditionalists from this list. Despite the impingement of law into them, they tend to be seen as issues which rightly concern churches and even as issues upon which governments might properly consult specific churches before legislating.

Because of this danger it is important to put my own position as clearly as I can at the outset. I will argue that churches do have a crucial role to play in society on moral and social issues. Despite the pluralism of society at large and despite the comparative decline of the churches I believe that it is entirely legitimate for churches to seek to embed Christian values into that society. Indeed churches can already claim more success than is sometimes imagined in transposing these values into a supposedly secular society. I will argue in the next chapter that the Welfare State, professional attitudes, penal policies and even academic scholarship are redolent with transposed Christian values in Britain today. Biblically consonant values in tension lie at the heart of the Christian ethics and are still at the centre of some of Britain's most important institutions. Further, I will argue that churches have a highly distinctive role in society in that almost alone they combine active pastoral care with a continuing concern for moral insight and the bases upon which this insight is founded. Whilst most other institutions are concerned primarily either with essentially non-judgmental care or with public policy and moral or social reform, churches unusually are involved in both.

However it is precisely this distinctive role which places constraints upon churches in their attempts to reach agreed positions on specific moral and social issues. Their deep and entirely legitimate concern for moral insight encourages them to seek such

agreed positions. Yet their active experience of pastoral care to individuals, in all their ambiguity, acts as a continuous constraint. Every
sensitive parish minister will be at once aware of the paradox here.
Moral considerations may convince the priest that divorce, abortion
and a whole range of other issues are less than Christian. Yet the
sensitive care of individuals who are divorced or who have had
abortions may convince the pastor differently. It is distinctly easier
to moralize in theory than it is in practice when the minister must
continue to be a face-to-face pastor to the individuals concerned.

This paradox affects all churches. It is only certain exclusive
sects that overcome it.[2] Sociologically, the latter can maintain a
pattern of moral purity which is impossible for churches. The
Jehovah's Witnesses, for example, are moral absolutists on a range
of issues. They may not participate in warfare, they may not vote
and of course they may not have blood transfusions. If individual
members do any of these things they will be excluded altogether
from membership. Moral purity can only be successfully maintained over a period of time by excluding those who deviate from its
absolute standards. No mainstream church in Britain today would
wish to impose such an exclusive policy. I will argue later that there
are some extreme situations in which sectarianism is the proper
Christian response. If society at large becomes sufficiently evil then
Christian institutions properly respond by seeking to purify their
membership. In contrast, churches are characterized by a membership which varies very considerably both in its moral attitudes and
indeed in its behaviour. These variations actually within the
membership itself of each church provide the raw material of the
paradox.

There are a number of ways that churches have developed to
cope with this paradox.[3] Those churches which are still committed
to an ethical method based upon natural law have developed
elaborate systems of casuistry. Moral principles themselves are
unchangeable, but within specific situations they may be found to
be in conflict with higher principles that must be preferred. Specific
situations may prove, on minute inspection, not to involve the
overall principles that at first seemed apposite. Or even, specific
situations may be tolerated temporarily although they are known
finally to be wrong. In all of these ways a church may maintain in
theory that morality is specifiable and absolute, yet in practice it
may condone or at least tolerate individual deviants.

Roman Catholic responses to contraception provide a very obvious example of this particular process. At first it appears that contraception as such violates the principle that every sexual act of intercourse should be potentially procreative. From this it would seem that sexual intercourse is not permissible for those who are known to be infertile, due either to some physical disability or to the age of the woman. It is clearly not permissible between those of the same sex or between those who never intend to have children together or even between couples when one of them has been sterilized. But such a rigid position fits ill with human behaviour even within the context of marriage. So in fact a moral position which seems to be so rigid in theory soon becomes modified in a number of crucial ways. It is not contraception as such which is forbidden but only certain methods of contraception. The safe period, spontaneous sterility and the impediment of age are deemed to be 'natural' and are thought not to vitiate the principle of potential procreativity (homosexuality, on the other hand, is still deemed to be 'unnatural'). Even when elaborate medical means are used to chart the safe period its use for sexual intercourse is still thought to be 'natural'.

Not surprisingly many Roman Catholic couples in Britain today by-pass their church's moral teaching on contraception altogether. It is even arguable sociologically that Pope Paul VI's Encyclical *Humanae Vitae*, which in 1969 reaffirmed this traditional teaching so decisively, did more to activate dissent amongst practising Roman Catholics than any other recent event.[4] Anyone with Roman Catholic friends will be well aware of the sentiment frequently expressed by them than an unmarried priesthood is in no position to tell married couples what they should do in their own bedrooms. What was intended to be a reaffirmation of tradition and an impediment to growing permissiveness has rather become an obstacle to many Roman Catholics and an encouragement to question tradition. Empirically it would seem that most Roman Catholics in Britain today do not abide by their church's teaching on contraception. Having questioned this, it may not appear too surprising that they also use abortion facilities in proportions commensurate with non-Roman Catholics.[5]

In this situation every Roman Catholic priest is faced with a paradox. He is expected to maintain his church's moral teaching on contraception, but he is confronted with active churchgoers who do not accept or abide by this teaching. If he takes a rigorous line in confessional or even in conversation his parishioners may leave, look elsewhere, or perhaps just avoid confessional or private conversation. In reality a system that appears from the outside to be absolutist soon becomes tempered by pastoral practice.

Those churches which are committed to the moral teaching of the Bible rather than to natural law exhibit the same paradox. Biblical exegesis takes the place of casuistry. It becomes a matter of contention, for example, whether the sixth commandment refers to homicide or to murder, or whether St Paul prohibited all forms of homosexual relationship or simply homosexual intercourse, or whether Jesus disallowed divorce in all circumstances or just in non-adulterous circumstances.[6] If Christians lived in a world from which all homicide, homosexuality and divorce had been eliminated, even amongst their fellow Christians, the outcome of this exegesis would be less crucial. The harder interpretation could simply be accepted. But of course they do not. And the very variety of practices within even relatively conservative churches forces the paradox upon them. So in North America, for example, even churches which regard themselves as biblically conservative are ambivalent about divorce. Despite some of the obvious biblical injunctions against divorce the phenomenon is too widespread in society at large for churchgoers themselves to be unaffected. Ironically it has been the fundamentalist churches which have provided some of the most enthusiastic support for the divorced Reagan against the monogamous, twice-born Carter.

Those churches which are traditionally more eclectic in the sources from which they draw their moral insights have an additional constraint. It is not simply the pluralism of their own membership which conflicts with clear moral precepts but also the pluralism of the sources from which these precepts are to be drawn. In reaffirming that in Anglicanism revelation, reason and experience are traditionally interwoven, the Church of England's Doctrine Commission in their recent *We Believe in God*[7] frankly recognize this to be the case. On certain moral and social issues there may be a degree of unanimity across the various sources of the Bible, of the churches' tradition, of current rational enquiry, and of the experience of worshipping communities today. Yet we can be fairly sure that on the majority of issues there will be no such unanimity. The multitude of positions represented in my own *A Textbook of Christian*

Ethics is far more indicative of pluralism than of unanimity.

Further, unanimity is not even a guarantee of validity. Until the late eighteenth century Christians might have been remarkably unanimous that slavery is not antithetical to Christianity and that capital punishment is a proper and necessary resource of the state. Until recently they might not have seen racism and sexism for the evils they obviously are for many Christians in Britain today. For Christians until the age of Constantine non-participation in war was assumed to be the proper Christian moral behaviour. Whereas for many subsequent Christians, until very recently, pacifism was regarded as an eccentric, and perhaps disloyal, response to war. Even twenty years ago the Dominican Ebehard Welty saw little place for Roman Catholics who wished also to be pacifists.[8] Yet today the Dominicans at Oxford are some of the most important catalysts of the Christian peace movement in Britain.[9] Unanimities change.

The effect of these two observations – about pluralism and about changing unanimities – might be to paralyse moral decision-making altogether. That is certainly not my intention. I have argued with passion for specific causes elsewhere and regard it as crucial that thinking Christians should do so. Individuals within churches, groups of like-minded individuals within churches, and indeed groups of like-minded Christians across churches, should I believe offer a much higher public profile. It is incumbent upon us to argue that Christian faith is relevant to the whole of life and to seek to transform society in its light. Size is not important here. Indeed Wilberforce and his fellow 'saints' provide a very obvious example of how a small, but thoroughly determined, group of Christians can effect immense social changes. Such changes may not halt a process of decline in the churches, but decline itself should not preclude Christians from attempting to change society. It is also right that Christians should discuss and debate moral and social issues with other Christians who take opposing views. Churches can be an important public forum in areas of moral debate. Given their distinctiveness in combining a concern for moral insight with active pastoral care they have every reason to believe that they can offer society an important role model. What they have less reason to believe is that they can arrive at and then present to society a series of specific moral and social positions as properly their own.

Yet that is exactly what church assemblies and synods confronted by their own radical decline seek to do again and again. In the process they attempt to overcome the evident pluralism both of their own membership and of the resource from which they draw. In short, they attempt to ignore the constraints that should be evident to any parish minister and to anyone carefully relating theory and practice within the churches. Although they make an increasingly sophisticated use of the social sciences, they by-pass complexities in moral decision-making. Within the context of a university, moral conclusions are properly reached only after much struggle and difficulty. And once they are reached the academic who is working alongside colleagues from other traditions soon becomes aware that unanimity is seldom reached on moral and social issues. Choices have to be made by the individual which can seldom be fully replicated in others. Academic theologians hopefully learn from each other and refine the reasons behind their choices. If they are honest they are aware that these choices could have been made otherwise. The moral individual does make choices. The moral individual even argues for these choices. But the moral individual avoids making the same choices for others.

A crucial distinction is essential at this point. I am not claiming a one-to-one relationship between church decline and an increasing tendency of church assemblies and synods to espouse specific moral and social positions. Universal churches also exhibit the same tendency, as do churches confronted by a radically evil state (e.g. Nazi Germany or Apartheid South Africa). Church decline is not the only stimulant of this tendency and the tendency is not its only symptom. In less pluralistic societies – united by mediaeval hegemony or by modern totalitarianism – this tendency may not be a symptom of decline at all. It only becomes such in a situation in which both society at large and church membership are themselves characterized by pluralism. In this situation the tendency can be seen as a natural, but I believe misguided, attempt to overcome pluralism.

An analogy might be taken from recent British politics. It is arguable that one of the central problems facing the British Labour Party today is the increasing affluence of a majority of the population. Of course there are still (and perhaps increasing) sections of British society which suffer from multiple deprivation. Nonetheless, the eighty per cent of the eligible population who are in employment now have a degree of affluence which may not make them natural Labour Party supporters. The Labour Parties of Australia and New Zealand have recognized this by seeking to combine social concern with surprisingly monetarist economic policies. However, important sections of the British Labour Party are convinced quite oppositely that increasingly specific socialist policies are required for electoral success. Confronted by declining support amongst the electorate, they actually seek a return to ideological purity.

It might at first seem that the United States Roman Catholic bishops offer an example counter to my thesis. The 1980s have seen them being prepared to make courageous and widely praised moral and social challenges. These challenges have been made in a manifestly pluralistic society and have signalled a new preparedness of the bishops to engage in overtly political issues. First on the sensitive nuclear issue in *The Challenge of Peace: God's Promise and Our Response*[10] and then on finance in *Economic Justice for All: Catholic Social Teaching and the US Economy*,[11] they have moved in the direction of increasing specificity. Yet they remain a numerically strong church. Here pluralism and specificity do not seem to be correlated with decline.

The example is in reality more confusing than this might suggest. Simply on the basis of decline, it is true that the US Roman Catholic Church is still strong compared to any British church, yet it is certainly an institution facing radical decline. Whereas in 1966 sixty-six per cent of all US Roman Catholics regularly attended mass, by 1976 only forty per cent did.[12] Non-Roman Catholic attendance has remained at about forty per cent: it is Roman Catholic attendance which has radically declined. Further, a careful reading of the bishops' challenges suggests that they lack the specificity[13] and stridency of the South African *Kairos Document* (to which I shall return in the next chapter). Finally, Roman Catholic sociologists are beginning to take the empirical evidence of pluralism seriously[14] and to maintain that, despite such attempts to encourage moral/social unity Western Roman Catholicism is itself actually becoming more pluralistic.

Joseph Fitzpatrick's *One Church Many Cultures: The Challenge of Diversity*[15] provides important evidence of this final point. In general he is sympathetic to the aims of the US bishops. For him, 'the letter on the arms race was a significant event in American

Catholicism. It represented for the first time an official statement of the official Catholic Church challenging, on moral grounds, the policies of the US government.' Both letters provide an affirmation that 'if the spirit of the gospels is to be "inculturated" in American society, some fundamental changes must be made in American policy and in the American way of life'.[16] Yet, having argued that, his book shows at length the considerable diversity of American Catholicism – European immigrant, followed by Americanized middle-class, followed by Hispanic immigrant, types of Catholicism – which makes representative moral and social claims considerably more problematic. In this situation the bishops themselves become one voice amongst many, even within American Catholicism. A theory of moral unity is not supported by such empirical diversity of practice.

The General Assembly of the Church of Scotland provides an instructive example of this gulf between theory and practice on social pronouncements. If anything it has been even keener than the General Synod of the Church of England to make pronouncements on a range of moral and social issues. In both bodies the debates have often been stimulating and have contained many intelligent contributions. Both bodies have active academics contributing to them and both have access to the expertise of a number of significant social scientists and political theorists. Yet both belong to churches which have been declining for a century with a tendency to seek unanimity despite the evident pluralism of their own membership and of the resources from which they draw. In the case of the Church of Scotland the issue of abortion over the last three Assemblies has highlighted the difficulties that this tendency creates.

The morality of abortion was debated vigorously in the General Assembly in the 1960s especially in the build up to the Abortion Act (1967). Frank Gibson, the secretary of the Church of Scotland's Board of Social Responsibility, still regards the issue as 'the supreme question'.[17] The deliverance of the Board to the 1985 General Assembly made the following recommendations, all of which were accepted;

1. That the Church be asked to reaffirm the biblical and historic Christian conviction in the sanctity of all human life and that, from the beginning, the foetus is an independent human being, made in the image of God.

2. That the Church be asked to conclude from this conviction that the 'inviolability of the foetus' (1966 report) can be threatened only in the case of risk to maternal life and after the exhaustion of all alternatives.

3. That the Church be aware of the practical difficulties which confront those in the medical profession in the exercise of their work particularly through pressure of time and encourage continued discussion both within and outwith the profession of the ethical issues involved in cases of termination.

4. That the Church be asked to consider ways in which alternatives to abortion can be put to those with difficult pregnancies, and support provided for them, by the encouragement of voluntary agencies and where appropriate by clearly rendering existing counselling facilities available to those in need, also by providing accommodation and other practical assistance where necessary.

5. That local congregations recognize and develop their opportunity for providing a healthy environment in which young people may develop caring and responsible relationships, involving all members of the Christian family, and in which handicapped children or adults would find a role as equal members.

6. That the Church commit itself to securing a review of the 1967 Abortion Act.[18]

These recommendations contain elements of both moral insight and pastoral care. The Church of Scotland has a long history of sustained pastoral care and indeed still teaches the subject in a number of universities in a professional manner seldom found in England. The links that it has with the medical profession and with voluntary agencies, assumed in the third and fourth recommendations, are real and well developed over the years. Nevertheless, the claims made in the first two recommendations are not shared by all members of the church as became very apparent in the 1986 General Assembly debate. Commenting on this a year later the Board's deliverance to the General Assembly noted:

On reflection it has to be admitted that the thinking behind this statement could have been expressed with greater clarity. For example, it is not clear what is meant by 'from the beginning' – when is 'the beginning'? – and the word 'independent' could be taken to imply physical independence of the foetus, which was not what was intended. The phrase had meant to assert the individuality of the foetus from the moment of fertilization. After much controversy in 1986, the General Assembly voted to adopt a modified position which, it was said, would allow abortion to be carried out in other than the life-threatening circumstances defined above, but nevertheless still on very restrictive grounds.[19]

Now the difficulties clearly emerge. Much in the abortion debate hangs upon a decision about 'the beginning' of a life which is fully human. It is difficult even to describe the various choices that must be made without at the same time prejudging the issue. At times the deliverance seems to recognize this as it sets out the various stages in the initial development of the foetus – the development of gametes, fertilization, implantation, differentiation – made even more complicated if the later stages are also added. Anyone who has tried to analyse competing ethical arguments about abortion will realize that this whole area is a minefield, with consider-able pluralism evident within moral philosophy and even within Christian ethics. After reviewing some of these competing views the Board finally prints in bold type its 'unanimous agreement' that from the time of implantation 'the foetus has to be regarded as a person'. My point is not that this decision is necessarily wrong. If one is to say anything moral about abortion some decision has to be made. Rather it is that this is a contentious decision and one that will represent only some views even within the Church of Scotland.

Equally contentious at a theological level is the assumption running through all the deliverances about the 'sanctity' of life. Presumably all Christians, and indeed all theists, hold that life is God-given, but this need not be quite the same as claiming that life is either sacred or sanctified. These last claims seem to ascribe holiness to human life which some theologians would maintain belongs more properly to the Creator that to the creature. Some Christian ethicists have even claimed that the concept of the sanctity of life belongs more properly to Hinduism than to Christianity. Again it is not necessary to mediate on this debate. It is sufficient to note that the claim to sanctity is contentious. It is also a claim that appears less frequently in debates about the morality of war. Finally for some it contains suspect specyist assumptions: it presumably implies that it is only *human* life that is sanctified.

The clear aim of the Board, expressed in the sixth recommend-ation of 1985, is to effect a change in the Abortion Act (1967). This is expressed more forcefully in 1987 in terms that signal strongly the moral assumptions of the Board:

> The General Assembly of 1966 decided that the basis for legislative provision for legal abortion should be that 'the continuance of the pregnancy would involve serious risk to the life or grave injury to the health, whether physical or mental, of the pregnant woman'. The Board believes that this should remain unchanged as the basis of the Church's view of how the law should stand. While Christian opinion on this subject is spread across a broad spectrum, and while the Board recognizes that Christians disagree on a number of important matters ... we are united in believing that the Church of Scotland should seek the co-operation of other Churches to work for a change in the law which would embody this principle. Thus the Board recognizes the importance of a consensus approach within the Church and believing that the effective change will only be achieved by a radical revision of the law on abortion; and call on members of the Church of Scotland and other Christian people to join in repudiating the scandal of a law which permits abortions on other than the most serious grounds.[20]

Not only does this quotation show clearly the strong moral presuppositions of the Board, it also displays a very evident contradiction. It wishes to uphold both a consensus approach to the abortion issue within the Church of Scotland and to call for a radical revision of the Abortion Act. The animated debate at the General Assembly in 1986 already demonstrated that there is no consensus upon the issue within the church and certainly not a consensus about a radical revision of the Act. Herein lies the problem for the Board. It wishes to stir the Assembly into taking united action together with other church bodies even whilst recognizing, at least in part, that the abortion issue remains contentious and that Christians remain seriously divided on it.

Simultaneously the Board sponsored a printed debate about abortion between six theologians, five of whom are ministers within the Church of Scotland. Published under the title *Abortion in Debate*[21] it presents opposing contributions under three headings; 'The Biblical View', 'The Foetus as a Person', and 'The Traditional View'. Each contributor expresses his or her (Elizabeth Templeton is regrettably the only female contributor) view and then is allowed a brief response to the opposing paper. This excellent book serves to highlight some of the central differences evident amongst thinking Christians on this issue. Unfortunately it also cuts away the ground from the Board's hope for a consensus. It is not at all clear that Elizabeth Templeton, Kenneth Boyd or Ian Fairweather, all of whom are known through their publications as thoughtful ethicists, are in favour of any radical reform of the Abortion Act.

However, it might be held that although it is true that theologians as such are divided on the issue of radically reforming the Act, the membership of the Church of Scotland at large might be more favourable. Here again the Board provides evidence that this is not the case. In a separate and highly commendable exercise it sponsored a major survey of attitudes of both churchgoers and non-churchgoers in Scotland – published by the Board in 1987 under the title *Lifestyle Survey*.[22] From this it emerges that Church of Scotland members are distinctly more pluralistic on the issue of abortion than are Roman Catholics. Indeed, they are almost as pluralistic as the general public. Whereas forty-three per cent of those without church membership considered that abortion is 'a matter entirely for the persons concerned', and thirty-five per cent of Church of Scotland members felt the same, only thirteen per cent of Roman Catholics concurred. Of those who felt that abortion is 'always wrong', forty-four per cent were Roman Catholics, eight per cent were non-church members and only six per cent were Church of Scotland members. This hardly provides convincing evidence of a strong antagonism to abortion from average Church of Scotland members. Even when the most committed members of the Church of Scotland are isolated unanimity is still absent. Nineteen per cent of this group do believe that abortion is 'always wrong', yet twenty-one per cent believe it to be 'a matter entirely for the persons concerned'. On moral issues such as abortion congregations seem to be at least as divided as theologians. They are just as aware as Elizabeth Templeton of the discontinuity between the church as it could be and the Church as it actually is. She expresses this as follows:

> We are called, too, to manifest the new kind of community we hope to become, where 'unwanted child' would be a contradiction in terms, and where even the awful distress of a family

with congenitally diseased children might be transformed by unfailing support and creative care. But until we can offer that, concretely, our central affirmation must be that as we participate in the messiness, pain and frustration of an untransformed world, we are held and involved in the love and forgiveness of God ... if we are incarnational Christians, we flesh out the judgment of God not by being judgmental, but by bearing in our own lives the cross; by destroying the platitudes of our self-righteousness, and by suffering the moral ambiguity and complexity of the actual world. To withdraw to the apparent safety of ethical blacks and whites, to tell others what to do without sharing the insideness of their predicament, is to retreat from the generosity of the Christian Gospel, and the flexibility of grace.[23]

If this position is taken seriously it is difficult to see that it could possibly sponsor a radical reform of the Abortion Act. Even if it were a remote possibility that a concerted attack upon the Act by all of the Scottish churches together would effect a change in the law – and this certainly cannot be assumed – the desirability of such an attack can be seriously questioned on both consensual and theological grounds. On this, as on many other moral and social issues, there is no evident consensus amongst either theologians or church members generally. Even if there were such a consensus, it must be asked whether church assemblies should seek to change laws which impose moral standards on others (in the case of slavery the answer today is clearly 'yes'). But in the absence of a consensus such attempts to change the law must appear even more misguided. Once again, individuals and groups of like-minded individuals within and across churches are free to speak and act in ways that would be unjust and sometimes impossible for representative church bodies.

I have taken the issue of abortion at length because it provides an important test-case for my argument. At first sight abortion is an issue that should be the object of church pronouncements. During the 1960s, prior to the Abortion Act (1967), church bodies were widely consulted by Parliament on the issue.[24] Further, it is an issue which has politicized the Roman Catholic hierarchy in Britain. For obvious historical reasons they have been less active on socio-political issues than the leaders of other churches in Britain. However, abortion seems to have changed this situation. Even though individuals might dissent from the positions of particular churches, most might concede that it is entirely proper for churches to be so involved and so specific. For this reason the fact that church assemblies and synods find it so difficult to reach any consensus on abortion is all the more instructive.

There might even be widespread agreement that although abortion necessarily involves legislation, since it must be permitted in some form or not, it also involves family and sexual issues which are properly the concern of the churches. Like pornography and divorce, a cluster of moral, religious and social concerns are traditionally thought to be involved here – concerns which should be the object of specific church teaching. Each is thought to offer a threat to traditional family life and the Christian life-style which is still the basis of much of British society. Each contains a conflict between the freedom of the individual and the pattern of family life of the majority of the population. So it might seem entirely proper that churches as churches should make specific pronouncements and then seek to shape the law of the country. In theory there might be considerable support for the Church of Scotland's Board of Social Responsibility in its attempt to do just this. Yet in practice this attempt has been confronted with enormous difficulties. There is no consensus amongst either theologians or members generally within the Church of Scotland.

These difficulties increase very considerably if an issue in social morality without family and sexual implications is taken. Some of my academic work has been on the ethical issues surrounding nuclear deterrence. Although I have also been considerably interested in abortion, nuclear deterrence now has priority. For me, the scale of horizontal and vertical nuclear proliferation, in a century which has seen some fifty million people killed in war, makes this 'the supreme question'. However, it has also become abundantly apparent to me that Christians are thoroughly divided on the legitimacy of nuclear deterrence, and that church assemblies and synods work within tight social constraints on the issue. I am also aware that this is not an issue which is always thought to be 'a matter for the churches'. Indeed, even the modest positions on nuclear deterrence that some church bodies have taken have been strongly resented by some.

The Church of Scotland's *Lifestyle Survey* again highlights these differences. Fifty-one per cent of Church of Scotland members in the survey believed that nuclear weapons are 'an effective deterrent against war', whereas thirty-six per cent found them to be 'morally unacceptable'. Roman Catholics were significantly more anti-nuclear: only twenty-one per cent thought them to be an effective deterrent, whereas a surprising sixty-six per cent considered them to be morally unacceptable. Those who professed no church membership whatsoever were actually more morally antagonistic to nuclear weapons than Church of Scotland members. In this group forty-six per cent deemed them to be an effective deterrent and forty-five per cent to be morally unacceptable. Even when the most highly committed members of the Church of Scotland are isolated from the survey it is still forty-seven per cent who found the weapons to be an effective deterrent and only forty-two per cent who believed them to be morally unacceptable. Age would seem to be a more important factor in shaping attitudes towards nuclear weapons than membership of the Church of Scotland. Amongst the young, thirty-nine per cent believed the weapons to be an effective deterrent (fifty-six per cent amongst the elderly), whereas forty-eight per cent considered them to be morally unacceptable (thirty per cent amongst the elderly). From this it would seem that critical church attitudes towards nuclear deterrence in Scotland have been more influential upon (or more representative of) Roman Catholic than Church of Scotland members. The latter are, once again, thoroughly divided on a moral and social issue.

Theologians are also divided on the legitimacy of nuclear deterrence. One has only to compare the celebrated report of the working party under the chairmanship of the Bishop of Salisbury, *The Church and the Bomb*[25] with the response edited by Francis Bridger, *The Cross and the Bomb*[26] and that with my own *The Cross Against the Bomb*,[27] to realize that this is the case. The divisions are deep and the debate has done nothing to eliminate them. Even more conservative Christian traditions are beginning to admit this. In this respect Myron S. Augsburger and Dean C. Curry's recent *Nuclear Arms: Two Views on World Peace*[28] is a remarkable achievement. Both theologians come from an evangelical, biblical tradition: Augsburger is a Mennonite from the Washington Community Fellowship and Curry is at Messiah College in south-central Pennsylvania. Yet they clearly hold opposite views on the consonance of nuclear weapons with Christian ethics. Augsburger is much influenced by his fellow Mennonite John Howard Yoder and derives from a christological reading of the Bible the principle of 'the way of non-violent love as always our first premise in relation to any conflict'.[29] He argues at great length that the principles of proportionality and discrimination in just-war theory are infringed by any potential use of nuclear weapons. He concludes with the claim that as 'Christians, our commitment is to Christ and to global enrichment by the rule of God, to the evangelization and discipling of people of all nations, and to the removal of all evils that rob people of the privileges of life and faith. Nuclear weapons, as the greatest destructive evil, must be rejected and removed from the human scene'.[30] Curry dissents, not from these evangelical commitments, but from his deductions about the potential use of nuclear weapons. He maintains, in contrast, that some uses of nuclear weapons are consonant with the just-war principles of proportionality (since they are sometimes no more damaging than 'conventional' weapons) and discrimination (since their tactical and limited use can be deployed against primarily military targets). I cannot pretend to agree with Curry's analysis or even with Augsburger's subordination of Christian ethics to evangelization. But I do consider it a mark of growing maturity that evangelicals can publicly unpack their differences over moral and social issues.

The difficulties that church bodies have over an issue such as nuclear deterrence is not simply caused by the pluralism of their membership or of their theologians. They are deeply constrained by social factors resulting from their relationship to society at large. If it is a central difference between a church and a sect that the church is an inclusive institution whereas the sect is exclusive in both its membership and its doctrine, this constraint is apparent. The close relationship of a church to the society in which it exists precludes it from differing too sharply with that society. The most obvious constraint upon churches in their socio-political role is that they themselves are a part of the social process. That is, opinions on public issues within churches and even the 'official' opinions generated by church assemblies and synods are demonstrably shaped by the very societies they are seeking to mould. On major social issues, such as those of war and peace, it is difficult for churches as churches to sustain views which are markedly different from those in society at large. On issues which relate to the family and sexuality some distance is certainly possible, as the Roman Catholic Church has demonstrated during this century. Although, even here, this may be more a difference of theory than of practice. However, on social morality distance becomes increasingly difficult. In effect this means that it is very difficult for churches consistently to maintain a unilateralist, let alone a specifically pacifist, position on nuclear weapons.

To a sociologist the decision of the February 1983 General Synod of the Church of England not to accept the unilateralist position of *The Church and the Bomb* was entirely predictable. It was at best highly unlikely that an assembly of the established church could adopt a position on a major social issue which was opposed both to current government policy and to general public opinion. It was only slightly easier for the non-established Church of Scotland's General Assembly to adopt a unilateralist position: it has proved far more difficult actually to sustain this position. Despite the fact that both churches are generally tolerant towards unilateralists even amongst some of their leadership (so long as they remain a small minority), the position is not a serious policy option.

It is not that there is actually a consensus in either church about the coherence of British independent nuclear deterrence. In this respect the contributors to *The Cross and the Bomb* are, by their own admission, rather unusual at the moment in claiming that the policy is both coherent in itself and consonant with theological principles. In the introduction the editor argued:

> Since the NATO decision of 1979 to modernize nuclear systems in Europe, the renewed rise of unilateralism has contained a vocal Christian element which has presented its stance as the only legitimate one for Christians to follow. This has been reinforced by a flow of theological publications and public declarations by churches. The present authors seek to refute this claim by arguing a case which they believe to be no less moral, but which points in the direction of deterrence and multilateralism.[31]

From this it is apparent that unilateralism *is* thought to be moral and legitimate for Christians to follow (even though it is not the only Christian option) and that nuclear deterrence is only 'no less moral'. It is also evident that the authors felt themselves to be on the defensive and arguing against the prevailing theological ethos. None of this might seem surprising until it is remembered that they were writing *after* the February 1983 General Synod decision overwhelmingly to reject unilateralism.

However strong the moral or theological case for unilateralism it would seem unlikely that assemblies or synods in the national churches could consistently espouse it. Their relationship to society at large effectively precludes this. Indeed, the history of Christian attitudes towards war and peace suggests that Christians generally since the age of Constantine have found it difficult to sustain moral positions at odds with society.[32] If pacifism was once the norm for Christianity, it has been the position of a tiny minority of individuals and sects since Constantine. The social constraints against it are exceedingly powerful.

These constraints work at several levels. At the level of the individual church member, he or she is simultaneously both a church member and a citizen. Members of a few introversionist sects (such as the Exclusive Brethren, or, more dramatically, the Amish in North America) might be able to by-pass public opinion and pressure, but members of churches can seldom escape. If individuals' churches tell them not to use certain methods of contraception, but everything in the public domain insists that they can and even should, it is hardly surprising that a gulf develops between theory and practice. At the level of 'official' decision-making a degree of social determination also becomes apparent. It is not difficult for anyone skilled in group processes or in organizational sociology to see how these factors work in church assemblies and synods. This is not to belittle these church bodies. It is simply to recognize that they are plainly human institutions subject to social constraints. As such they pose a problem for those seeking to discover their proper public role. This role will be the subject of the next chapter.

3

Social Action Beyond Decline

So far I have argued that declining churches face a number of temptations. In the areas just considered two opposite positions may be identified. The conservative position is to argue that Christians should ignore social and moral issues and concentrate instead on specifically 'religious' issues. Church growth and evangelization are seen as the essential task of the churches. Concern for moral and social issues are viewed as deflections from this essential task. The radical position is to argue instead that declining churches should strive more effectively to change society in increasingly specific ways. Churches can be mobilized on specific moral and social issues and can together offer a real challenge to a pluralistic society. They should seek to present to a sceptical world an ethical perspective which is distinctively Christian.

Over the next two chapters I will offer an alternative to these two positions. Against the conservative position I will suggest five ways for Christians in Britain today to be engaged in moral and social issues. It is surely far too simplistic to believe that Christianity can by-pass moral and social issues. In practice those who claim that it can usually mean that it should by-pass *certain* issues – nuclear deterrence, capitalism, unemployment, etc. They seldom mean that it should by-pass issues such as pornography and abortion. The five ways that I will suggest all take into consideration the social constraints that featured in the previous chapter.

Against the radical position my own scepticism about churches as churches being able to reach a consensus on many moral and social issues will already be apparent. The desire for a distinctively Christian ethical perspective on specific issues is certainly understandable in a pluralistic society. Yet the evidence seems to suggest that it is more an idealistic hope than a real possibility. It would of course be wrong to construct a vision of what churches could do simply on the basis of what they actually do. A sociological view of the churches should never be allowed by Christians simply to replace a theological view of the churches as related to the kingdom of God. Nevertheless I believe that there should be some relationship between theory and practice. If it is constantly maintained that churches ought to be doing one thing and yet the empirical evidence suggests that they are too constrained actually to do it, then there surely is room for doubt.

Both the conservative and the radical positions have a tendency to ignore obvious evidence within ordinary church life. The conservatives forget that, in practice, they are concerned about certain moral and social issues (even if these issues are different from those that concern the radicals). There are obvious moral concerns present within the New Testament. And there is a long and remarkably successful history of evangelicals effecting moral and social changes. In the last century social activism was more a characteristic of evangelicals than it was of non-evangelicals within the British churches. Radicals, on the other hand, have a tendency to idealize Christian action and to ignore the social constraints that surround it. Nor are they very good at asking searching questions about the effectiveness of stark moral positions. Sometimes it can even seem more important for them to make radical moral and social pronouncements which have no prospect of implementation, than to adopt effective compromises. Like radical politics, radical Christianity can at times appear more concerned with moral purity than with actually changing the world. Yet the expressed intention of both forms of radicalism is precisely to change the world.

If the conservatives regard church growth and evangelization as central to their role, the radicals are often suspicious of institutional churches altogether. Even whilst deriving their salaries from institutional churches, they may appear to show little concern about their demise. And even whilst suggesting radical and far-reaching action for churches to engage in, they may be impatient of the institutional structures necessary to effect and sustain this action. It is quite remarkable how little serious research has been undertaken into the type of social structures that are the prerequisite of successful moral and social action within the churches. Sociological enquiry has been extensively used to map changes within churches and changes within their social context. It has only rarely been used to suggest more effective church structures for the future.[1]

It is hardly surprising that the two groups are so polarized within the British churches today. Both are responding to the decline of the churches, yet their response is quite opposite. The conservatives tend to feel that they alone are concerned about Christian growth and the effective survival of the churches. They provide an increasing proportion of all ordinands and sustain many of the most active Sunday schools and youth fellowships. They tend to look askance at what they see as the politicization of Christianity and the transformation of evangelism into social work. The radicals, in contrast, are often appalled at the 'churchiness' of the conservatives and the degree to which they appear content to ignore social deprivation. They tend to regard the convervatives as excessively individualistic, being apparently more concerned with individual salvation than with the broader network of social relationships and structures. In short, they tend to see conservatives as simplistic and lacking in any real concern for society at large.

The two groups are analysed with much skill in Robert Towler and A.P.M. Coxon's *The Fate of the Anglican Clergy*.[2] On the basis of Coxon's research on Church of England ordinands in the 1960s and early 1970s they argue that conservatives and radicals are becoming increasingly polarized. They are even distinct culturally: they tend to read different books, enjoy different music and have quite different forms of social life. Their understanding of the nature and function of the church is quite opposite, and the ministry they expect to operate within it is at considerable variance. At present the conservatives are clearly on the increase, but Towler and Coxon suggest (perhaps rather wistfully) that in the long-term the radicals will form the main focus of ordained ministry.

It is more than possible that ordinands tend to exaggerate differences within the churches. This is especially the case within the Church of England since it alone segregates ordinands into colleges of differing forms of churchmanship. These colleges must serve to reinforce such differences far more strongly than the university faculties within which Church of Scotland ordinands are entirely educated. However, once they experience the realities of parish life they may lose some of these differences. Nevertheless, they still exist, especially when churches are perceived to be declining. Polarization may be a common feature of institutional decline.

In advancing an alternative to these two positions I need in this chapter to consider five ways that British Christians can effectively engage in moral and social issues. In the next chapter I will turn to the topics of church growth and evangelization. The five ways may be termed: individual prophecy, group prophecy, sectarian prophecy, transposition of Christian values, and moral praxis. They represent a spectrum of possibilities. Some offer a low tension with society at large and others a high tension. Some are concerned with large church bodies and the first simply with the individual. Further, they are not necessarily mutually compatible. Indeed, there is every prospect that individual and sectarian prophecy will sometimes be at considerable odds with the social activity of large church bodies. Yet together they give the lie to the notion that Christians should eschew moral and social issues.

In the classical literature of sociology a sharp distinction is sometimes made between the individual prophet and the priest.[3] The prophet is thought to be a lay figure who acts on the basis of a personal calling. Prophets can at times be socially disruptive and iconoclastic. If they are associated with communities at all they are communities of disciples dependent on the charisma and authority of the prophets themselves. They can be agents of radical social change, either by challenging existing forms of religion with some new religion or by seeking to restore existing religion to its pristine condition. Priests, on the other hand, are seen as essentially conservative, cultic functionaries. Their authority is derived not from some personal calling or revelation but from the church that they seek to serve. Their role is to maintain a rite and to sustain a congregation involved in this rite. They are more concerned with building community than with challenging society. They are unlikely to act as agents of social change, since their role is to conserve an existing form of religion rather than to replace it with a new or radically renewed form of religion.

This contrast is deliberately drawn in its starkest form. In reality parish clergy will be aware that they do not function wholly as priests in this sense. They are concerned with renewal, at least, and do use the language of vocation to depict their ministry. Yet the contrast does call attention to an emphasis that is a part of their experience. It is difficult to function for long in most congregations without becoming aware of the tensions inherent within sustaining a community of worshippers.[4] A relatively homogeneous congregation may present fewer tensions – for example a student chaplaincy or a city-centre evangelical or anglo-catholic church. But most congregations contain within them people of a variety of political and moral convictions. They may not even be united in liturgical terms. Within Anglicanism there is still a sharp divide between those who habitually attend an early morning communion service and those who attend mid-morning family communion or even late morning mattins.[5] Within such 'communities' the clergy themselves and the buildings within which they function may be two of the most important unifying factors. The effect of this is to make it very difficult for clergy to act as iconoclasts or agents of radical social change. They may themselves sometimes talk as if they have a prophetic role in society, but in practice it is seldom a role that is very evident.

Viewed from a sociological perspective, the clergyman in Britain today is the object of tenacious stereotypes. At a superficial level these emerge in cartoons and television comedies. Yet at a more profound level every parish clergyman soon becomes aware of pre-formed public expectations. These take many forms. They are partly related to social behaviour, evident when people apologize to clergy for swearing, feel awkward when they encounter them in pubs, or express outrage when they engage in hunting or shooting wildlife (but not, paradoxically, fishing). They are partly related to uniform. The dog-collar, which for the clergy themselves may simply be thought to be a means of introduction and identification, becomes for the public a pervasive symbol and signal to modify behaviour. It is no accident that clerical dress assumes so important a role for the clergy even when they claim that it does not.[6] Those of us who have regularly to choose whether we are to be perceived primarily as clergymen or as university lecturers (or whatever) soon become aware of the symbolic potency of the dog-collar. Those who are freshly ordained are also well aware of this. And implicitly other clergy are as well. If once it was customary for clergy to wear dog-collars whether they were working or not, today they can choose if they are to wear them on train journeys (or wherever) and may now feel conspicuous if they do.

Social stereotypes of clergy today are even applied ecumenically. If once it was imagined that only the Church of England clergyman was perceived as a 'clergyman', today this is certainly not the case.[7] Clergy themselves have confused boundaries by dressing across denominations. Even within the Church of Scotland the 'Roman' collar is frequently seen and within parts of the Church of England black is no longer the fashionable colour (although luminous green is). Women across various churches are experimenting with clerical styles of dress and bishops do not always use the distinguishing colour of purple. Allied to this, parish clergy within the Church of Scotland, the Church of England, the Episcopal Church, and even the Roman Catholic Church, are faced with very similar public expectations. All report tensions in relation to public expectations about baptisms and church weddings. All face the demands of folk religion and civil religion in some form. And all are aware of their minority status in a pluralistic society.

I will return to some of these features in the next chapter. For the moment it is sufficient to notice the contrast between the figure of the radical prophet and the constrained role of the British clergy. All societies operate constraints, especially upon those who have highly visible, institutional roles. Social constraints can be overcome, but only with considerable difficulty.

By distinguishing the individual prophet from the priest the sociologist is able to point to some of the difficulties that confront the prophet. Those who wish to challenge society can usually expect to meet strong resistance and public disdain. The history of the socially conscious evangelicals of nineteenth-century Britain well illustrates this. Josephine Butler, who is buried only six miles from my parish, provides a very remarkable example. Single-mindedly she campaigned for thirty years against the contagious diseases acts (requiring women suspected of prostitution in certain ports to have compulsory venereal inspections), first in England and then within Europe. She befriended and cared for individual prostitutes despite her own genteel background as a farmer-landowner's daughter. And she spoke and campaigned continuously at even quite violent political hustings. Most remarkably she did all of this whilst being the wife of a Church of England clergyman who was headmaster of Liverpool College and then a residentiary canon of Winchester Cathedral. Her own account of her work makes it clear that she felt a strong moment of 'calling' to undertake it and that she regarded it as a form of obedience to her evangelical commitments.[8] Not surprisingly, however, her work is only now being recognized by the church to which she belonged. For most of her contemporaries she must have appeared embarrassing and inappropriate, or perhaps very much worse.

Prophecy requires a great deal of single-mindedness when confronted by a hostile society. The courageous individual who is an effective prophet must be prepared to defy convention both within society and even within the churches. All churches have a tendency afterwards to routinize prophecy and to depict it as an essential corrective within a holistic understanding of the church. They thus seek to accommodate prophecy within an ecclesiastical economy. Yet when they are actually confronted with living prophets their reaction is seldom so generous. Like most institutions, churches in reality are more concerned with conservation than with radical, and of course risky, social change. Precisely because they are themselves a part of the social process they are unlikely to endorse radical social challenges. Viewed with hindsight prophecy appears as an essential means of combating the instinctive institutional conservatism of churches. In this sense individual prophecy is essential. Yet at the time radical prophecy is seldom actually popular.

Of course it is easier to identify the past contribution of individual prophecy to society and to the churches than it is to identify the present contribution. Herein lies a problem for the churches today. The very individuals that they most disparage today may be the recognized prophets of tomorrow. The risky and self-authenticating nature of individual prophecy renders it unacceptable to contemporary churches. It is worth recalling that the evangelicals who so successfully campaigned in the last century to change laws on slavery, prostitution and child labour in factories, also enforced sabbatarianism.[9] Yet individual prophecy is one of the most important ways that Christians can engage effectively in moral and social issues. Individual Christian prophecy may sometimes change society in ways that appear impossible for churches as churches.

Prophets may gather communities of disciples around them. Josephine Butler was no exception. Her husband was undoubtedly a strong source of support and she campaigned alongside other feminists and politicians, some of whom were Christians and others not. Prophetic communities can act as important social sustainers in an otherwise hostile world. In this respect they operate no differently from other deviant sub-cultures. They are 'deviant' for a sociologist in the sense that they deviate from the norms dominant in society at large. They are sub-cultures in that they form a network of support and encouragement for those who hold norms which deviate from those which are culturally dominant. For the sociologist delinquent gangs have much in common with prophetic communities. They differ though in that the latter are concerned to change society whereas the former may simply be intent upon resisting society.

Groups or communities with a prophetic task can be found both within churches today and across churches. They form a second major way for Christians to engage effectively in moral and social issues. Christian CND forms a very obvious example of this type of action. Its membership is drawn from a wide variety of Roman Catholic, Anglican and Reformed churches. Those who belong to it are naturally committed to both CND and to Christianity in some form, but otherwise they may be quite disparate. Within the churches from which they are drawn the dominant ethos is still antithetical to the unilateralism or nuclear pacifism of CND. In this respect they are a deviant sub-culture within the churches. They also wish to be identified as 'Christian' and thus to be seen as distinct from general CND members. It is not an all-encompassing group or community. Members usually belong to other Christian communities or congregations in which their anti-nuclear views will be minority views. Nonetheless, most will believe that it is important that such views should be represented even within churches that do not overtly support them.

Group prophecy is able to achieve a measure of immunity from social constraints. If it seems impossible for churches as churches to sustain a unilateralist position on nuclear weapons, it is certainly possible for individuals within churches to join with others who are convinced of unilateralism. Even bishops have recently felt able to declare their membership of Christian CND. This of course signals a change that may already be taking place in society as a whole. The 1987 General Election did not endorse unilateralism. Yet by being so strongly espoused by the second largest political party, unilateralism may be losing some of its deviant status. It is far less conceivable that British bishops today could openly declare membership of the Gay Christian Movement. Some prophetic groups are evidently considered to be more deviant than others within the churches. However, all provide social support for their membership – thus reducing outside constraints – before seeking together to change attitudes within the churches.

Within Roman Catholicism the religious order has for many centuries sometimes been allowed a degree of deviance, especially on moral or social issues, which would be unacceptable in other groups within the church. The current Dominican involvement in the peace movement fits this pattern and contrasts sharply with the difficulties that Monsignor Kent has had as a diocesan priest. Franciscans especially have for long been allowed considerable forms of eccentricity. Many sociologists have argued that religious orders act as essential channels of deviance in a seemingly uniform church.[10] Whereas amongst Reformed churches deviance has often resulted in sectarian schism, within Roman Catholicism it has tended to be contained instead within religious orders. They can thus serve to represent moral and social positions which are not open to the church as a whole. In this sense they too can be prophetic in ways less possible for the Roman Catholic Church at large.

It is important to recognize that group prophecy is often engaged in conflict. It may be conflict that is tolerated by the churches or even encapsulated by them within separate orders or societies. Yet it is conflict nonetheless. Churches may even contain within themselves diametrically opposed prophetic groups. The Church of England now contains both the Anglican Pacifist Fellowship and the group Shalom, sponsored by the Bishop of Oxford to defend nuclear deterrence on theological grounds. Neither group may represent the dominant ethos within the Church of England at present. If unilateralism is a minority position, then so might be a theological (as distinct from a purely pragmatic) defence of nuclear deterrence.

Far from regarding this as unfortunate, I believe that it brings into the open a far more mature and realistic understanding of the churches. Conflict is not always helpful, but it surely can be an important part of learning, especially about crucial moral and social issues. Conflict openly expressed makes clear the pluralism within particular churches, whatever their dominant ethos. It unmasks attempts to establish uniformity as exercises of coercive power rather than consensus. And it mirrors far more closely the process of moral decision-making apparent in modern academic theology.

If group prophecy was more firmly established within the churches, there might be fewer calls on general assemblies and synods to make specific moral and social pronouncements. On an issue such as abortion, it would be more clearly recognized that there are deep divisions of opinion amongst Christians, even amongst those

belonging to a common tradition. Abortion is an extremely perplexing issue, made more perplexing still by the need for clear legislation on it in a society containing both Christians and non-Christians.
Christians are right to be concerned about it and should be encouraged to relate their Christian beliefs to it as fully as they are able.
They are right also to campaign for their views, once formed,
alongside other like-minded Christians. They are right, too, to seek
further support across denominations. Yet they are mistaken if they
believe from this that they should require their own churches to
speak with a single voice. An expectation of moral uniformity may
not be a sign of moral or Christian maturity.

Group prophecy presupposes a level of compliance with socially
conformist churches. Churches are broadly tolerant towards the
prophetic groups that operate within them, and individual members
of the groups themselves continue to be members of the churches.
Implicit within this relationship is a recognition of the pluralism
and inclusivity of the churches. The individual simultaneously
seeks to persuade others to accept a particular moral position, yet
recognizes that churches rightly contain some who may never be so
persuaded. So, an individual committed to SPUC may appear quite
convinced that abortion is 'murder'. As a member of SPUC he or
she will be deeply involved in a moral and political crusade. Yet as a
member of a pluralistic church that same individual will still share
communion with those having quite different convictions. Indeed,
others may observe that few individuals who claim that abortion is
'murder' actually treat those who have had abortions as murderers.
Once again there is a very obvious difference between stated theory
and observable practice.

This compliance is noticeably absent from the third way for
Christians to engage effectively in moral and social issues – namely,
sectarian prophecy. Some sociologists distinguish between churches
and sects on the basis of their relative inclusivity or exclusivity.[11]
The church is inclusive both in its membership and in its doctrines.
It does not make rigorous distinctions between members and non-
members and seldom attempts to exclude individuals for 'heresy'.
The sect, in contrast, is exclusive in both membership and doctrine. The sect typically does not tolerate nominal members, requires its members to be clearly identifiable, and does exclude
those it deems to be 'heretics'. Another way that some sociologists
make this distinction is to argue that sects have a high tension with

society at large, whereas churches have a very low tension and a strong tendency towards social conformity.[12] Not all sociologists would accept these distinctions. Recently some have argued that the polarity between churches and sects is less apparent in declining churches in a pluralist society.[13] Examples from sects or cults such as Scientology would also seem to suggest a membership which is in many respects middle-class, intelligent and socially conformist.[14] Nevertheless, most might still agree that it is only the sect which is capable of the sort of exclusivism to be found in the Jehovah's Witness Movement. In contrast to this the Church of England or the Church of Scotland are still eminently inclusive.

The finer points of this debate are not relevant here. It is sufficient simply to notice this broad difference. For the present purposes sectarianism will be seen as a label more suited to the Jehovah's Witness Movement than to these more inclusive religious institutions. Viewed in this way sects are not given to compliance. If prophetic groups still operate within inclusive churches, exclusive sects do not. The moral absolutism that characterizes Jehovah's Witnesses is so absolute that they frequently refuse to identify it in any moral terms whatsoever.[15] Of all religious organizations today the Jehovah's Witness Movement is amongst the most committed to thoroughgoing pacificsm. Individual members in Nazi Germany, in parts of Africa and in the Soviet Union have suffered strong persecution for refusing military service.[16] Yet the Movement tends to reject the pacifist label. It belongs to a political framework which the radical eschatology of the Movement has rejected. In turn, this rejection has tended to bring the Movement into even sharper conflict with totalitarian political regimes. This is clearly not a compliant form of prophecy.

Sectarian prophecy demands total allegiance. There is no question of individuals simultaneously belonging to conformist churches. The exclusive sect is able both to specify and, more crucially, to enforce specific moral and social positions. Those who deviate from these positions must be excluded if the moral purity of the sect is to be maintained. If, for instance, abortion is identified as 'murder' then those who have abortions must be treated as murderers. There is no attempt here to balance moral orthodoxy with pastoral concern. The individual must choose whether to be one of the saved or to join the damned. Soteriology overwhelms the niceties of pastoral practice. The type of casuistry which tempers a strict adherence to natural law within traditional Roman Catholicism, or the exegesis which tempers biblical literalism within Reformed Christianity, is absent here. Injunctions on moral and social issues are to be obeyed without exception.

On the issue of pacifism a clear difference is evident between Jehovah's Witnesses, Amish Mennonites, and modern Quakers. Superficially it might seem that Quakers are the most conspicuous pacifists. Even in the First World War, Quakers were sometimes granted exemption from active military service.[17] Conscientious objection has proved considerably more difficult for other groups (particularly those which are not religious) to establish to the satisfaction of military draft boards. Further, amongst younger British Quakers today peace issues sometimes assume more importance than ostensibly religious issues. Nevertheless, modern Quakers are predominantly middle-class and highly educated. Exclusivity is if anything more anathema to them than to members of national churches. As a result Quakers who are thoroughgoing pacifists, Quakers who are selective pacifists, and Quakers who are not pacifists at all, have continued membership of the same fellowship.[18] Representative pacifism remains a strong feature of the Quaker Movement, but it has nothing like the consistency and absolutism of that to be found amongst the Jehovah's Witnesses or amongst the Amish communities of North America. As a result it may even be misleading to identify the representative pacifism of the Quakers as sectarian prophecy. The label more typically applies to the other two movements.

Sectarian prophecy in its most typical form is a response to a society which is perceived to be evil. Its intolerance is an expression of a prior social denunciation. Those who adopt this way of engaging in moral and social issues do so because they are convinced that social conformity would betray the very cause to which they are committed. The price for this position is social marginalization. Few societies enjoy being denounced. Most react by attempting to marginalize, and perhaps even persecute, those who act in this way. The prophetic sect in turn devises elaborate mechanisms to protect itself against society.

The crossover from group prophecy to sectarian prophecy is very critical. In both specific moral and social positions are espoused and mutual support is given by fellow members to withstand counter-pressure from society at large. Both are concerned to effect social change and are well aware of the limited ability of pluralistic churches to achieve this. Yet they differ crucially in their analysis of the evil of society and in their own willingness to exclude members who think differently. For sectarian prophecy, society is too evil to be tolerated and church compliance must itself finally be judged to be evil. As a consequence, individual members cannot be allowed to maintain membership of churches which are party to such evil. Group prophecy, in contrast, by allowing its members to maintain their church membership, implicitly accepts a level of pluralism which belies any wholehearted denunciation of society that might also be made. In practice, group prophecy is usually a form of sustaining moral and social positions in a manner that does not intend to challenge the central aims of society.

A very important example of this crossover in process can be seen in *The Kairos Document*[19] produced in 1985 by a group of South African theologians and churchmen. In arguing for a prophetic theology the document produces a devastating critique of both 'state theology' and 'church theology' in South Africa today. It is already established as one of the central texts of the churches in the 1980s and will surely be a focus of debate for some years to come.

The document clearly fits the first requirement of sectarian prophecy. It regards the South African state as thoroughly evil and denounces churches which attempt to reach accommodation with it. 'State theology' is seen as 'simply the theological justification of the *status quo* with its racism, capitalism and totalitarianism. It blesses injustice, canonizes the will of the powerful and reduces the poor to passivity, obedience and apathy'.[20] The state itself is evil:

> The oppressive South African regime will always be particularly abhorrent to Christians precisely because it makes use of Christianity to justify its evil ways. As Christians we simply cannot tolerate this blasphemous use of God's name and God's word. 'State theology' is not only heretical, it is blasphemous. Christians who are trying to remain faithful to the God of the Bible are even more horrified when they see that there are Churches, like the White Dutch Reformed Churches and other groups of Christians, who actually subscribe to this heretical theology.[21]

Because the state is so thoroughly evil *The Kairos Document* believes that any church accommodation with it is no longer justifiable. Even the sort of accommodation more typical of the English-speaking churches in South Africa is disallowed. It identifies this as 'church theology', which 'in a limited, guarded way ... is critical of apartheid. Its criticism, however, is superficial and counter-productive because instead of engaging in an in-depth analysis of the signs of our times, it relies upon a few stock ideas derived from Christian tradition and then uncritically and repeatedly applies them to our situation'.[22] So, this kind of theology pleads for 'reconciliation' in a situation in which 'it would be totally unChristian to plead for reconciliation and peace before the present injustices have been removed'.[23] And it pleads for non-violence 'in a blanket condemnation to cover the ruthless and repressive activities of the State and the desperate attempts of the people to defend themselves'.[24] 'Church theology' basically lacks an adequate understanding of 'politics and political strategy':

> Changing the structures of a society is fundamentally a matter of politics. It requires a political strategy based upon a clear social or political analysis. The Church has to address itself to these strategies and to the analysis upon which they are based. It is into this political situation that the Church has to bring the gospel. Not as an alternative solution to our problems as if the gospel provided us with a non-political solution to political problems. There is no specifically Christian solution. There will be a Christian way of approaching the political solutions, a Christian spirit and motivation and attitude. But there is no way of by-passing politics and political strategies.[25]

Even although the document maintains that there is no specifically Christian solution to the problems in South Africa, it is clear that it does believe that there are very specific actions which churches should be taking there. As a result of its understanding of prophetic theology it sets them out in detail, including acts of civil disobedience, believing that 'the church must now take sides unequivocally and consistently with the poor and the oppressed'.[26]

Herein lies the difficulty for *The Kairos Document*. The authors are fully aware that 'the Church is divided'.[27] Yet they believe, as the title of the document suggests, that 'the moment of grace and opportunity' has arrived and that 'the situation is too critical' now in South Africa for continuing divisions amongst Christians. Indeed, 'we sit in the same Church while outside Christian policemen and soldiers are beating up and killing Christian children or torturing Christian prisoners to death while yet other Christians stand by and weakly plead for peace'.[28] They refrain from suggesting that this overcoming of division amongst Christians in South Africa must actually be coerced. But they come very near to it. They are evidently in transition. South African Christians who condone, or at least accommodate, the evil of apartheid are still called Christians, but the logic of the document militates against this.

The situation is so reminiscent of that which gave rise to the Confessing Church in Nazi Germany that it is surely just a matter of time before those involved in *The Kairos Document* call for a more exclusive approach to Christianity. For my part I believe that it is right that they should do so. For me the apartheid regime is indeed so evil that Christians who accommodate it are deeply tainted by it. If such a position is accepted, the churches in South Africa have no option but to turn in a sectarian direction. By adopting sectarian prophecy they can witness more purely against an evil regime. Yet of course they must pay the price – increasing marginalization and possibly even persecution by that regime. Their only comfort in such a situation is that other Christians have been there before.

In describing this situation of extreme crisis, it will be evident to many that Britain today is not in the same situation. Society at large may contain evil elements within it, but it is not itself thoroughly evil. Even in terms of *The Kairos Document* the *status quo* of British society cannot be wholly identified with 'racism, capitalism and totalitariansim'. Without quibbling with the grouping together of these three – isms, in Britain today each is tempered by important counter-structures dependent upon deeply held underlying values. Of course there is still racism in British society and there are sections of the population which remain intractably racist. Yet the prevailing ethos is anti-racist, there are laws which attempt to suppress racism, and overtly racist political parties gain little electoral support. Further, British society is not simply capitalist. The welfare state is still an important feature and all the major political parties insist that they do 'care' for the poor and underprivileged. Compared with North American capitalism the British economy remains a mixed economy despite the advent of monetarism. And democratic elections remain central to British society. The prevailing ethos is thoroughly anti-totalitarian and politicians who hint at extra-parliamentary activity are generally viewed with deep suspicion.

If all this sounds rather complacent, it is certainly not intended to be. My point is not that racism, selfish capitalism and coercive totalitarianism have been eliminated from British society. Nor is it that there are no other social evils to be combated in Britain today. On the contrary, in the fifth chapter I will give strong support to *Faith in the City*. Rather it is that British society is not to be confused with the thoroughgoing evil of South African apartheid.

Once this distinction is made, sectarian prophecy may not appear the most appropriate way for British Christians to engage in moral and social issues. A fourth way is through the transposition of Christian values.[29] Of all the ways of engaging in moral and social issues this is the most elusive, but, over time, it may also be the most important. A judgment about this depends upon a set of assumptions about the role of shared values in sustaining an ordered society. It suggests that underlying Christian values, rather than specific church pronouncements, have played a decisive role in shaping British society and that they are still implicit within many of our institutions. Even if these values are largely invisible to us or, if visible, their Christian roots are generally forgotten, they are nonetheless vital to the quality, if not the survival, of British society today. Within such a set of assumptions it is still a primary social role of the churches to sustain these values, to articulate them when necessary, and to seek to transpose them further into the structures of society.

John Habgood, the Archbishop of York, is an able advocate of this approach. In *Church and Nation in a Secular Age* he shows that he has carefully read some of the recent literature in the sociology of religion and is well aware of numerical decline within the British churches. At the outset he states that 'no discussion of Christianity in Britain can ignore the numerical weaknesses of all the churches, a weakness in which the Church of England fully shares. Nor can it ignore the fact that much of what is left of the historic national role of the two established churches in England and Scotland, is now exercised in partnership with others'.[30] He also insists that 'Christianity is not just about values. Nor is its primary purpose to secure social stability, though this may in practice emerge as one of its useful functions. A faith reduced to this role, however, would have become as secularized as the society in which it is set'.[31] Yet, despite this, he does believe that British churches still have a crucial social role.

For Habgood the very pluralist nature of Britain today under-lines the importance of this crucial, but largely hidden, role. He believes that pluralism, within both society and the churches, has certain benefits. So he claims that, 'on the whole a complex society, representing many shifting and competing interests, is more stable than a simple one',[32] and that a variety of co-operating churches is preferable to a monolithic church with its tendency to polarize particular societies (for example, in Italy). However, pluralism, in itself, suffers from a central weakness:

On a very simple estimate of social order, stability might be thought to depend on the existence of at least some shared values. For most of the time it may be possible for people to work together on the basis of a tacit consensus, or even on the basis of a supposed consensus which hides the disagreements ... But there are occasions in the life of any group when the degree of consensus is tested, and it is then that there has to be an appeal beyond the particular interests represented to some higher legit-imating value or authority. But where does this reside? In a secular pluralist society shared values and recognized authorities are the fruits of consensus, not the basis of it. If there is no higher authority than the State itself, and if there are real and deep divisions which lead to a breakdown in the consensus, what then is to be done? ... Logically the conclusion seems inescap-able that a fully pluralist state, which was that and nothing more, could only survive by drawing from time to time on values outside its own commitment to pluralism.[33]

In such a situation the churches can play an important role. For Habgood 'the question what is it that enables a nation to hold together and function as a nation?' does have a religious dimension to it.[34] Further, churches being local and voluntary, are 'small enough to enable those who belong to them to see the difference they are making' and are thus able to provide 'the main life-chance for people who feel more and more dominated by the bigness and impersonality of the modern world'[35] Finally, at the level of the individual politician or policy-maker, religion has a crucial function in forming people with the necessary altruistic motives. Thus, 'the kind of people who are called upon for advice in controversial matters, or who help to restore the integrity of public life when things go wrong, are usually people who have themselves been nourished by some source of excellence outside the political system'[36]

As Archbishop, Habgood is convinced that the Church of England still uniquely represents all of these different levels of social integration. Because of its established position it can minister to leading politicians and policy-makers. Indeed, *Faith in the City*, despite initial government hostility, is having an unusually large political influence. And it is now clear that *The Church and the Bomb*, despite its rejection by General Synod, was widely read by active politicians. Further, because of its open-ended local presence in the community, Habgood believes that the Church of England can still reach people beyond its formal membership. Through these channels it can yet provide central values in an otherwise pluralist society. He even sees a potential influence in the General Synod debate on *The Church and the Bomb*: 'the actual differences between Christian ethical judgments need not matter so greatly ... those who see no easy answers, may have cause to be grateful that a mature Christianity can contain these differences, and thus help to prevent the political debate polarizing into sterile confrontation'.[37]

Most recently he has sought to put these convictions into practice by chairing the group which produced *Changing Britain: Social Diversity and Moral Unity*. The report seeks to uncover the role of core values in the stability of society and the ways that these values are generated. The roles of the family, education, the media, and political parties are each inspected, but finally it is the role of the churches that is identified as crucial. The report argues that

> Britain is an old culture, rich in institutions (the churches amongst them) and with a great deal of cultural and institutional interpenetration. That is our history, our fate in one sense, and we cannot change it. This is the past on which successive futures are and will be built. It is not possible either for church or society to wish the other away, and it is not permissible for Christians to withdraw from debate about public values and simply leave others unchallenged in their pronouncements.[38]

Changing Britain, with Habgood, believes that the Church of England has a key social role:

> Any Christian church, and especially a national one, courts particular dangers but it ought also to have special gifts, qualities and insights to bring to the issues this study has considered:

breadth of vision, the ability to handle complexity and to live with polarities, moral concern rooted in basic principles rather than detailed prescriptions, wide pastoral contacts and commitments, a recognized place both in the voluntary sector and as an integral part of national life, a sense of responsibility for the whole nation constantly tempered by broader international and religious perspectives, a realistic appraisal of our human capacity to deceive ourselves and serve our own interests, a message of hope in the face of failure, cynicism and despair – all these and more.[39]

The authors are, of course, aware that the Church of England does not always live up to this detailed remit. There is an element of ambiguity about whether they are depicting this role as it is, as it was, or simply as it should be. Whichever is the case, the role clearly envisages a national church and relates less obviously to some other denominations in Britain.

Indeed, Habgood's own claims for the uniqueness of the Church of England's social role have understandably not been warmly received by all. They sit somewhat uneasily alongside his initial recognition of the partnership of other British churches. Reformed critics have additionally criticized his tendency to overlook individual or group prophecy.[40] And there is also some ambivalence in his work about whether he assumes that religion in some form is essential for the survival of society or simply that religion contributes importantly to the quality of society. It is really only necessary to claim the latter. Wars of aggression, collective greed and even despotism can effectively unite societies. But naturally they all change the quality of those societies. It is sufficient to claim that Christian values have historically played an important role in shaping British society (scarcely a very contentious claim). And then to argue that the very quality of British society would be diminished if it is now to be based on contrary values. This of course is a contentious claim. Yet it might be one that Christians generally, and perhaps many others in society as well, would be prepared to defend.

A striking endorsement of this approach appears at the very end of the 1987 *Lifestyle Survey* sponsored by the Board of Social Responsibility of the Church of Scotland. The academic consultant, Alex Robertson, a senior lecturer at Edinburgh University in social policy, argues that Christian values are fundamental to the welfare state.[41] He is aware from the survey of the tendency for 'the lifestyle, attitudes and goals of members of the Church of Scotland – with their emphasis on sexual morality, their tendency to restrict their social circle and the contentment they appear to feel in surveying their own life histories – to be governed more by the desire to avoid doing what is bad, than by a concern to pursue more positively what is good'.[42] But he strongly believes that things could be otherwise and that church members could be prompted to think more broadly. He concludes as follows:

> But how, in the final analysis, do we deal with the problems raised by the apparent failure of the Welfare State to match up to the vision proposed by Titmuss? Can social policy become an instrument not only for attempting to promote social justice but also for the integration of individuals into a caring society? This is perhaps the most difficult task of all. Public provision of services alone apparently cannot be relied upon to achieve this goal. Nor does even the ethic of professionalism render individuals immune from selfish and competitive individualism when they feel their interests to be affected. The Christian vision is ultimately one of a society of caring equals who are free to express their individuality in the pursuit of Divine Grace. It is the motivation relating to that final goal that perhaps provides the only proper and lasting basis for a caring society. It is to that the Church should probably look for its most distinct, lasting and effective contribution.[43]

This challenge to the churches is all the more remarkable because it comes not from a theologian but from a leading social scientist. It is almost as startling as the claim of the late Paul Halmos in his *The Faith of the Counsellors*,[44] that the Christian values of *agape* and care are essential features of effective counselling – however much secular counsellors (of which he was one) sought to disguise or deny it. There may be a growing recognition amongst social scientists that values are essential to a whole range of social activities and structures. These include the welfare state and professional standards, but they also include medical, penal, and business ethics. They may even include the standards of diligence and intellectual integrity implicit within the academic world. Ironically, it has sometimes been social scientists who have then reminded others that values in all of these areas have at least some of their roots in the

Judaeo-Christian heritage. Further, *Faith in the City*, both in England and in Scotland,[45] has provided a number of leading social scientists with a platform to combine social analysis with moral and pastoral concern. Within the constraints of formal academic life that in itself is unusual.

This suggests the final way for churches to engage in moral and social issues, which I will term moral praxis. As the name suggests this way attempts to combine moral insight with pastoral practice. It may be one of the most distinctive features of the churches in pluralistic Britain that they still combine moral insight with a sustained effort to care. The inevitable precept of many caring organizations and agencies in a pluralistic society is that they must offer their care in a non-judgmental and non-moralistic manner. In a past society which assumed a high level of moral consensus, it might have seemed appropriate for doctors to offer moral advice to pregnant teenagers, drug abusers, alcoholics, etc. Today it certainly is not. A rigorous distinction must now be made between the private morality of doctors and their role in public. It is no longer thought appropriate for doctors to offer patients specifically moral advice, even on issues such as abortion. Nor is it thought appropriate for many others in caring roles to offer moral insights. In this respect the clergy are rather unusual. They are expected to care for the elderly, the sick, the lonely and the disadvantaged, yet they are also thought to be moralizers. I suspect, from my own parish experience, that some with marital problems may avoid the clergy for this very reason.

In contrast, the media especially are persistent moralizers. The tabloids present to their readers a remarkable combination of moral indignation at the sexual behaviour of leading figures, politicians and (if at all possible) clergy, with sexually stimulating gossip and photographs of television and film personalities. In a more sophisticated form, the intellectual press and television are also persistent moralizers. It is, for example, predictable that most articles and programmes about the natural world will conclude with moral injunctions against environmental destruction or pollution. And particular issues soon become subjects of moral crusades – child abuse, AIDS, Watergate, etc. Indeed it is an important feature of a free society that the media are allowed to moralize in these ways. However distasteful they may sometimes appear, in a democracy they function as an important constraint upon those who have power.

The media moralize but naturally they do not combine moral insight with pastoral care. They may seek to effect changes in the behaviour of politicians or of the public at large. They may even be amongst the most important carriers of paradigm shifts in moral attitudes. Feminism, for example, has attracted enormous coverage from the media, bringing it to the attention of millions who would not normally read books on the subject. There is much debate amongst sociologists about the influence of the media – about whether they directly cause changes in society or simply stimulate changes that are already taking place.[46] Whichever is finally judged to be the more likely, the media have little role in the pastoral care of those they seek to change. Whereas the caring agencies attempt to care without moralizing, the media moralize with few means to care.

In this situation churches now appear unusual in attempting to do both. Through the parochial system and through many formal and informal Christian caring agencies a great deal of pastoral care is still exercised in Britain. Amongst ordinands pastoral care today receives increasing, and increasingly professional, treatment. The literature on pastoral care has been transformed. This is in no small measure due to SPCK's Library of Pastoral Care, written very largely by those who have been directly influenced by the enormous resources of North American pastoral care and counselling. If once it was thought that pastoralia was a non-examinable and easy option, today theological students soon discover otherwise. In university faculties and departments, diplomas in pastoral care now have an established and tested place. And, amongst Edinburgh students at least, there is a strong demand for supervised pastoral placements. There is also very considerable interest in Christian ethics amongst these students. Again they soon become aware that Christian ethics is no easy option and that there is more to the subject than voicing moral prejudices. A serious study of Christian ethics inevitably involves them in a critical examination and comparison of differing ethical traditions within Christianity. Underlying values that are held in common across these traditions – or, more accurately, underlying values held in tension – are unearthed only with considerable effort.[47]

An approach to moral and social issues based upon moral praxis presupposes that both of these elements – pastoral care and moral insight – are vital and mutually related. It entails the conviction that pastoral care for the Christian necessarily involves a concern for underlying values. It also entails the corresponding conviction that moral discussions are inadequate for the Christian if they do not also involve pastoral care. Precisely because Christians believe that the world is related to a God made known in Christ as a loving and caring God, value and care should not be wholly separated. Care is an expression of value and value is not to be expressed without care. For the Christian, care is not merely a sociable act, it is a reenactment of, or a response to, our relationship to a caring God. And values are products of this relationship and arbiters of our relationships with each other. As a consequence, pastoral care becomes an important testing ground for values that are thought to be Christian. And Christian values, once tested, become important guides for assessing the quality of pastoral care.

I believe that moral praxis most nearly represents the approach to moral and social issues implicit within many parish situations. It is tempting to believe that the parish priest can also be prophetic, either as an individual or as a member of a group, actually within a parish. Yet in practice pastoral care militates against this. So, at one level I can be the author of *The Cross Against the Bomb*, but at a parish level I am a parish priest in the Borders who must take part annually in an almost wholly unreformed Remembrance Day parade. Before I came to the Borders I had never sung 'O Valiant Hearts'. Twelve years later, after several gentle hints to members of the local British Legion that perhaps it is less appropriate today than it was at the end of the First World War, I am still singing 'O Valiant Hearts'. Twelve years of pastoral care in a community that suffered as Japanese prisoners of war has taught me humility. Of course I still preach about peace. They would prefer me to preach about valour. Yet they too are concerned about peace, even if we might strongly disagree about the role of nuclear weapons in keeping peace. For me it has become essential to distinguish between the underlying Christian values that can unite us and the specific moral proposals that manifestly do not. If I were to impose the latter on the Remembrance Day congregation, members of it would rightly believe that I had destroyed our pastoral relationship.

Moral praxis may also represent best the approach that is in reality implicit within most British churches. Current concern about AIDS well illustrates this. So far there have been mercifully

few Christians claiming in public that AIDS is a divine punishment. Most realize the ineptness of such claims and have hesitated
before making them. Not least of the difficulties involved in them
is the extraordinary picture of a God who also punishes non-
promiscuous AIDS victims – spouses, babies, haemophiliacs, and
even rape victims. Yet, in so far as AIDS is related to promiscuity,
many Christians will also have felt some moral indignation. This
indignation may even have turned to anger when confronted with
HIV positive prostitutes who are still sexually active. For all of this,
the overwhelming Christian response so far has been that AIDS
sufferers are children of God who are in special need of care –
however they themselves actually contracted the virus.

This approach to AIDS is well in evidence in a remarkable series
of articles that appeared in *The Tablet* in the first half of 1987.
The Oxford Dominicans have again been active, with their Prior,
Timothy Radcliffe, arguing strongly for a compassionate approach
to AIDS sufferers, and urging readers to accept the conclusion of
the Spode Conference on The Catholic Church and AIDS: 'We
urge the members of the Church in our countries, laity and clergy,
co-operating where possible with already existing organizations, to
search for the most effective means of help, and we ask our bishops
to give their active support to this work of Christ; for it His Body
which has AIDS'. Jack Dominian argued that 'we must avoid
simplistic solutions. Faced with the crisis of AIDS it is urgent and
imperative that a sexual and marital morality based not on fear but
on personal love should be established in the Christian community.[48]
And the Jesuit James Hanvey, having written about AIDS in San
Francisco concluded his article as follows:

> Back in Britain, I have been struck by the brutality and the
> paranoia of the government's campaign, which does little to
> educate those who have the disease and those who care for them.
> I am saddened at the trivial nature of the 'moral' debate about
> 'safe sex' and 'condoms', avoiding the fundamental questions of
> compassion, justice and responsibility, in our country and others
> – especially Africa – which really test the quality of our society.
> But I am saddened most of all by the slowness of the Christian
> response. 'Don't die of ignorance', the government says. It seems
> to me that no one should die in ignorance of God's love. I
> wonder how we shall be judged.[49]

These specifically Roman Catholic responses are all examples of moral praxis. Each attempts to point to underlying Christian values, yet sets them firmly in a context of active pastoral care.

The emphasis of Kenneth Boyd from the Church of Scotland is somewhat different, but it is clear that he too is concerned to balance moral insight and pastoral care. Writing in the *Journal of the Royal Society of Medicine* he concludes his article as follows:

> The need at present is for public education not only to state the facts about AIDS, but also to embody a response to it which finds meaning in moral complexity. The complexity is that of a world in which the dead are mourned, the sick and dying cared for, sensible precautions against infection adopted, treatments for AIDS and a vaccine sought, and life and sexuality enjoyed, not desperately but steadily. Finding meaning in such moral complexity will not be easy; and in the end, tragically, society may not find it. On the other hand, the consequences of AIDS for future generations may yet be a deeper appreciation of the meaning both of human sexuality and of human solidarity. One of the early Christian fathers (Justin Martyr) argued that the purpose of baptism was 'to make us children of choice and understanding rather than of compulsion and ignorance'. The ultimate moral challenge of AIDS is not very different.[50]

The aim of moral praxis itself may not be too different. If declining churches are tempted to make moral decisions for people in a pluralist society, moral praxis in contrast encourages moral maturity. If declining churches are tempted to eschew moral and social issues altogether, moral praxis insists that moral values in the context of care are properly Christian. Moral praxis does offer the churches, even declining churches, a distinctive role in society. In a society which cares and moralizes, but separately, churches continue to offer moral insights and pastoral care together. Care is inevitably based upon values, but in a pluralist society they remain hidden. Churches, in contrast, are quite open about the source of their values. They should also remain open about their hope to transpose these values into the world. Large or small, declining or increasing, it is properly their business to transform the world.

4

Outreach Beyond Decline

Every parish priest will be only too aware of church decline in Britain today. Recording communion figures each Sunday, if weekly communion is our tradition, or general attendance figures if it is not, we are ever conscious of 'slide'. Perhaps our particular congregation seems to be withstanding decline. Perhaps we are temporarily encouraged by some increase or by the initial enthusiasm that can greet a new and more dynamic priest. Perhaps we are challenged by a new family in the congregation. Nonetheless we will still be aware that we are surrounded by an institution in decline and that this decline may yet be a feature of our own congregation. Perhaps we can maintain a congregation without decline for the whole of the time it is in our charge. Perhaps. Yet even here we are conscious that decline may await our successor.

This may seem to be a very bleak picture of contemporary ministry in Britain. Most priests would rather not speak so frankly. Decline so often appears as a sign of personal failure even to those who should know better. Most of us insist that 'success' should not be measured in terms of numbers. Yet we are still impressed by those who build up large congregations in churches that were previously on the point of being declared redundant. Most of us are well aware that the kingdom of God is not to be confused with institutional churches. We may even be aware that institutional churches in Britain have fluctuated numerically over the last four hundred years – with times of dramatic increase and long periods of slow decline. So it becomes difficult for us to avoid the temptation to search for signs that the present decline is about to be reversed. Possibly it is a slight improvement in the number of those offering themselves for ordination. Or perhaps it is a slight rise in

Easter or Christmas communicants. However slight the indication, it is easy for any of us to turn it into a sign that things are about to change.

It is possible that those clergy who are no longer actively engaged in parish ministry are less aware than their parochial colleagues of these feelings. If one has to face the same congregation week by week it is difficult to avoid them. Even those of us who have been trained sociologically are still aware of them as we count our congregations each Sunday. We are fully aware of the strength of overall social factors, yet we are tempted to regard the size of our congregation as an indication of the success or failure of our ministry. Decline threatens our ministry and our own status as ministers. Whereas increase validates our ministry and declares us to be successful ministers.

At least, that is how it frequently appears, if not to ourselves then certainly to our congregations. Increase or decrease are readily transliterated into success or failure, and ministers are judged accordingly. Indeed, the more conscious churchgoers become of the prevailing decline of British churchgoing, the more they may be tempted to make such judgments. If only they could find a young minister, if only they could find an evangelical minister, if only they could find a minister who visited regularly, if only they could find a minister who preached interesting sermons, if only ... Whatever the future conditional clause, the sentiments will instantly be recognized by those who attempt to minister to congregations conscious of decline. Within denominations that give the final responsibility for calling new ministers entirely to local congregations such sentiments can produce ironic situations. For example, it becomes very difficult for some who have served faithfully overseas for many years to find a charge in Britain, 'if only' because, by definition, they are no longer young.

These feelings run across denominations. When I first came to Scotland fifteen years ago there was less recognition than now that the Church of Scotland is an institution in decline. If analysed carefully Church of Scotland statistics show decline for all of this century.[1] However, whilst the communicant roll remained over one million the church was often thought to be relatively static. Comparisons with the Church of England encouraged this view. Churchgoing in Scotland is still approximately double that in England and a greater proportion of the adult population in

Scotland is actively involved in the churches. Further, the Church of Scotland has been far more rigorous than the Church of England in closing 'redundant' church buildings. If the membership of an urban church in the Church of Scotland drops below six hundred, it is at risk of being closed (a criterion that would decimate the Episcopal Church of Scotland).

However, once the communicant role of the Church of Scotland dropped below one million in the 1970s, a realization of decline became far more widespread. In reality the phenomenon was long-standing. A frank recognition of it took much longer. Similarly, amongst Roman Catholics such a recognition has taken longer than it has in the Church of England or in the English Free Churches. Irish immigration for much of this century has, amongst other factors, tended to boost Roman Catholic churches in Western Britain. In addition, churchgoing as a continuous custom has proved much better established amongst British Roman Catholics than it has within any other British denomination. Nevertheless, despite a reticence to release official mass attendance statistics, there is now a widespread recognition that Roman Catholic churchgoing is declining. Within Europe as a whole this decline has been apparent over the last twenty-five years.[2]

Some of the small sects are amongst the very few religious institutions in Britain today that are still increasing. Indeed, some sociologists have argued that it is small self-contained sects, which have built up barriers against a predominantly secular society, that will be the only religious institutions to survive in Britain in the future.[3] On this understanding, churches will either cease to function altogether, merging without trace into the general popula-tion, or they will become sects protecting themselves from society. In either event church decline is assumed to be an ineluctable process. If religion survives it will only do so as the pursuit of a tiny minority of the population. Further, it will necessarily be a minority that has effectively withdrawn from mainstream society. British sects may continue to increase in size and in number, as they are doing at present, but it should be remembered that altogether they represent less than one per cent of the population.

Recently a number of sociologists of religion have begun to question this scenario. Using a cyclical theory of religious institu-tions[4] they have argued that church decline has been a feature of a number of periods of European history. If the sixteenth century was characterized by religious ferment and enthusiasm, the seventeenth century and particularly the eighteenth century were less obviously so. The early nineteenth century was characterized by very considerable religious apathy which was sharply reversed towards the middle of that century. The twentieth century has again seen considerable decline from the high point of Victorian churchgoing. In so far as churchgoing and involvement in institutional churches is seen as an indication of 'religiousness' (and not all sociologists would accept this)[5], then it would seem that recent history has been characterized by a series of declines and occasional sharp rises.

A cyclical theory has been strengthened by those sociologists observing religious, and not simply Christian, phenomena outside Europe. Some have pointed to recent rises in religious fundamentalism, particularly in Islam in the Middle East but also in parts of North America. If once it was claimed by sociologists that secularization is an inevitable feature of the modern world, today this claim is made less frequently. Many had supposed that the process of Westernization or liberalization initiated by the Shah of Iran could not be reversed. They assumed that the traditional world of Persian Islam would fade in the clear light of secularization and that religion, as elsewhere in the West, would become a marginal pursuit. They might have assumed as well that the United States, the most advanced industrial society in the world, would lose its old proclivity to Protestant fundamentalism. The rise of the so-called Moral Majority does not seem to have supported such an assumption. Further, the continuing centrality of religious differences in the civil conflicts in Northern Ireland and the Lebanon have undermined the confidence of some sociologists in a theory of the inevitability of secularization.[6]

Paradoxically the seminal figures in the sociology of religion, writing at the high point of European churchgoing, all tended towards some theory of secularization. Despite their very considerable personal interest in religion, they mostly considered that the processes which make up modern, industrial society militate against religion remaining central to that society. Until recently a theory of secularization of some description was still held by most of those working within the sociology of religion. David Martin's challenges to the theory in the late 1960s were at the time regarded as innovative.[7] However, twenty years later it is Bryan Wilson who is unusual in still maintaining a theory of thoroughgoing secularization.[8] For most of his colleagues the evidence from Iran, the United States, Northern Ireland, the Lebanon, and even Poland and the continuing political role of the present Polish Pope, is at variance with secularization. The climate within the discipline has shifted very considerably – paradoxically in an era of European decline in churchgoing.

The effect of this change of climate is to put a large question mark against simplistic identifications of churchgoing decline with some inevitable process of secularization. I am afraid that sociologists have themselves sometimes contributed to this identification. It was one of the more remarkable features of Bryan Wilson's writings on secularization twenty years ago that he did just this. Despite his immense erudition as one of the leading sociologists of religion in Britain, his *Religion in Secular Society*[9] and his later *Contemporary Transformations of Religion*[10] both argued that statistics of church decline in Britain were evidence of secularization. They argued this despite claiming that the quite different patterns of high churchgoing rates in the United States were also evidence of secularization. Clearly the statistics were actually irrelevant to Wilson's secularization thesis[11] and it is significant that they have been dropped from his more recent writings on the subject.[12] Sociologists are frequently criticized for defying conventional wisdom, but in this instance sociological theory actually gave a spurious credence to the popular notion that churchgoing decline signals the demise of religion in society.

In much recent sociology of religion a far more complex understanding of religion in society is beginning to emerge. By focussing upon non-church forms of religion in Britain today many would now argue that religious practices and beliefs are far from absent. Britain is less a secular society than a pluralist society.[13] As I argued in the previous chapter, Judaeo-Christian values still play a crucial, and sometimes forgotten, role in shaping society. But any parish priest or minister will also be aware of their continuing civil and community roles and will know that many who seldom if ever go to church still consider the church to be 'theirs'. Indeed, part of the dilemma that confronts clergy in any of the major denominations is that people with apparently little or no church connection will request rites of passage. Some regard this as simply a vestige of occasional religious conformity.[14] My own experience as a priest suggests otherwise. Individuals will often force themselves to ask for baptisms even when they believe (sometimes, but not always, wrongly) that the clergy will be hostile to the request. Even when baptism is administered only at the Sunday eucharist, nominal churchgoers still bring their babies for baptism. I suspect that many clergy underestimate the degree of courage that is neccessary to do this.

If this more complex understanding is adopted it will soon become evident that it challenges a number of the responses to decline apparent within the British churches today. It challenges the belief that there is a direct link between 'successful' ministry and a full church. Little is as capable of engendering guilt amongst clergy as this. Most of us are not very 'successful' in this sense and yet we are tempted to believe that others are. It also challenges a number of approaches to evangelism and church growth. Perhaps the most seductive temptation for declining churches is offered by those 'successful' evangelical churches which still recruit members where others apparently fail.

One of the most persistent myths amongst some evangelicals is that all that is needed for the churches to increase is that they should commit themselves wholeheartedly to a staged evangelistic mission. The evangelical revivals of the last century provide the paradigm for this myth. Precisely because they seemed to be so successful in promoting church growth and in reversing the apathy of the previous century, it has been hoped ever since that they can do the same in the present century. Any who went to the Billy Graham missions in London during the 1950s and early 1960s will be aware of this hope. Mass evangelism could bring about mass conversion which in turn could fill the churches. In reality the situation was very different. Yet this has not discouraged others from attempting the same. Most recently in Edinburgh and a number of other cities a major advertising campaign featuring a picture of a rainbow and the message 'There is Hope' is being attempted. Evangelism is conceived as a mass phenomenon. A simple and direct message can convince the unconverted masses to become Christians again.

My own exposure to the various techniques and expectations involved in this came when I was a curate in the town of Rugby. Together with the other six curates (Rugby was still a key training parish in the late 1960s) I was persuaded that it was our duty to the diocese to take part in its major evangelistic campaign. We were assured that there would be no attempt to replicate the techniques of Billy Graham. This was to be a diocesan mission. And some of it was very memorable. Television stars were invited to preach and the obvious pop singers. Cuthbert Bardsley, the Bishop of Coventry at that time, preached with great power. Yet as the mission proceeded most of the evangelistic techniques that some of us feared came to be used. Individuals were invited to 'come forward', music was used to enhance emotion, and a simple gospel was presented with the hope of gaining 'conversions'. It became increasingly difficult to tell this mission apart from the Billy Graham rallies.

At two points I found my own antithesis towards these techniques temporarily unnerved. On the very first night our coach of parishioners approached Coventry off the motorway. To my surprise we were surrounded by a mass of other coaches. For a moment I thought that the lack of enthusiasm from the people of Rugby had been atypical and that others had succeeded where we evidently had not. We went together as a great convoy into the middle of Coventry. The diocese clearly was going to grow very considerably. Unfortunately as we neared the cathedral all but a very few of the other coaches turned off to the football ground. Coventry City were at home that night!

The other occasion came when members of the congregation were invited to 'come forward'. It had been suggested to each parish that some of their clergy and laity should act as 'counsellors' and that when the invitation came they too should 'come forward' to encourage others. With very great reluctance we did as we were told. Suddenly the cathedral came alive with people 'coming forward'. Perhaps mass evangelism really did work in a way that our pastoral form of ministry did not. As soon as we entered the reception area for those 'coming forward' we were to discover that this was not the case. Almost all of those 'coming forward' were counsellors! In my naivety I knew nothing of this technique and had been disconcerted by it as teenager at a Billy Graham rally. 'How', I kept thinking at that earlier occasion, 'could so many seemingly intelligent people possibly be convinced by that?' Now I knew.

We soon discovered that of those who eventually were 'referred' to us as having genuinely 'come forward' all were already regular churchgoers. Puzzled by this and lacking any insider's experience of previous evangelistic campaigns, we asked the parishioners involved why they had done so. It became clear that they regarded it as an act of solidarity with the whole occasion. Each exhibited a deep sense of religious belonging. So perhaps it really was a diocesan occasion after all. The hopes of evangelism, conversion and outreach were the dreams which disguised the more humdrum reality of local congregations coming together at the cathedral. What appeared to be proselytism was actually a reinforcement of denominational belonging.

Having discovered this my worry since has been for those antagonized by such campaigns. Regular churchgoers who are encouraged and perhaps even strengthened in their religious commitment in this way have already undergone a considerable amount of religious socialization. The symbols and signs that are presented to them have an existing location for them. They already have some experience in handling them. Apparently instantaneous conversion in reality is usually a lengthy process (known by anthropologists as 'liminality')[15] involving some social dislocation, a period of mental limbo, an identification with a new or renewed frame, and perhaps even an extensive re-writing of personal history. Yet the way it is presented so often in evangelistic campaigns is in terms of a simplistic and instantaneous choice. Indeed that is the way that many of those who claim to have been 'converted' learn to re-tell the account of their conversion. Like Augustine, who in reality appears always to have been zealously religious,[16] they learn to pin-point an exact moment of total change. Just as scientists are forced by the conventions of scientific procedure to stylize and systematize the accounts they give of their methods of discovery[17] (pure accident, for example, is not an acceptable method!), so some evangelicals learn to stylize and systematize their 'testimonies'. Many critical evangelicals are thoroughly aware of this, but the danger is that the more conservative may simply convince others that they themselves cannot become Christians.

Precisely because this process seems to offer 'success' in a situation of general church decline it is all the more seductive. Yet in an increasingly educated society it is based upon a paradigm that is simplistic and stylized. Its inadequacies were obvious to me as a teenager and have only been reinforced by my subsequent study of the sociology of conversion. The fact that some clearly intelligent people are convinced by it does not detract from this. In North America a number of highly intelligent minds have applied themselves to creationist theories. And in British universities conservative evangelical societies remain strong. Undoubtedly they appeal to some. However for others they may simply serve to reinforce a conviction that Christianity is to be rejected. A simplistic faith can be simply rejected.

Once again there is a gap between theory and practice. Conservative evangelical techniques seem to be 'successful' in the sense that they appear to be able to reverse the predominant British pattern today of church decline. In practice their successfulness is not so clear-cut. Even the phenomenon of well-attended evangelical churches in university cities may be misleading. They suggest that if only other churches could be like them then they too would be well attended. For ordinands they frequently offer a role model which can lead to deep disappointment later when they are confronted with the realities of non-eclectic congregations. By gathering students and others together in city-centre churches they give an impression of youth and vitality. Yet in the process they transfer these young people out of their local congregations or student chaplaincies. The success of churches such as Holyrood Abbey in Edinburgh, St Michael-le-Belfrey in York, or All Souls Langham Place in London, are obvious examples of this. I believe that such churches do serve an important function. Like student chaplaincies they can offer young people a theological perspective which is relatively free from the compromises of more representative parish life. But it is not to be confused with the function of local churches. Sociologically they are more akin to cathedrals than to churches and may serve their immediate parish area no better than most cathedrals do.

One of the most seductive evangelical responses to decline is offered by the Church Growth Movement. Particularly in the writings of Donald McGavran, it offers a theoretical and a practical challenge to declining Western churches. The strength of McGavran's position is that he draws on an unusually rich variety of empirical evidence from churches around the world. He shows a tough-mindedness which has gone little noticed outside evangelical circles and a preparedness to use both sociological and theological resources. His central work *Understanding Church Growth*[18] shows that he is prepared to subject evangelical techniques to critical scrutiny and to discard those that no longer serve their purpose in particular contexts. Few academics have given serious critical attention to his writings despite their very considerable influence upon the evangelical world. Perhaps they should.

McGavran recounts the origins of his distinctive perspective as follows:

My interest in church growth was first roused when ... a survey showed that 134 mission stations in mid-India (where I was a missionary) had experienced an average church growth of only 12 per cent per decade, or about 1 per cent per year ... The ten stations of my own mission, the India Mission of the Disciples of Christ, were not significantly different from the other 124. They had a staff of over 75 missionaries and a 'great work' – but had been notably unsuccessful in planting churches. In the town of Harda where my wife and I with six other missionaries worked from 1924 to 1930, not one baptism from outside the church occurred between 1918 and 1954 ... I present these few instances as typical of much mission effort. The churches and missions cited are not more blameworthy than others; indeed, I hesitate to call them blameworthy at all. They do good work. They bear witness to Christ. They teach and heal men, distribute powdered milk, and demonstrate improved agricultural methods. But they do all these things, and much more, while their churches grow, if at all, by baptizing their own children. It may be truly said that the ambiguous cliche 'splendid church and mission work, whether the Church grows or not' characterizes most churches and missions today – in America and elsewhere.[19]

McGavran seeks to reverse this position by making numerical church growth central to his perspective. Instead of regarding numerical growth, in the Western churches as well as in the Third World, as a secondary issue he regards it as the primary goal. He is not at all impressed by those who think otherwise:

Churchmen getting little church growth defensively declare they are not interested in it and do not want it. We are not afflicted by 'numberitis', they retort. We would not be so earthy or hungry for quick and easy results as to seek or count conversions! We are aiming at something much higher and nobler – like building Christian character. Manufacture of high-sounding phrases *which do not involve church growth* is a speciality in some quarters. One of the best came out of China some years ago. 'We are engaged', it ran, 'in building Christ into the foundations of China.' Under this broad and impressive umbrella a missionary doing almost anything could raise ample funds.[20]

In describing his own work, set out in great detail in *Understanding Church Growth*, he insists that 'from the beginning to end it assumed that quantitative growth of the Church was God's will and ought to be measured, depicted, discussed, and made the basis for evangelistic and missionary labors'.[21] For him quality will follow quantity. He even argues that those who place quality first 'are in effect advocating works of righteousness and substituting ethical achievements, the fruit of the Spirit, for the Gospel. Christians, when true to the Scriptures and to Christ, reject such legalism and insist that ethical achievement *grows out of life in Christ* and must not be made a prerequisite for faith in Him.'[22]

Although he believes that there are a few situations which are not capable of church growth, he maintains that they are exceptional. In these, 'resistance is too high, hostility too great, for men to obey or even "hear" the Gospel. There are counties and cities in almost every nation in which Christians can preach, teach, and heal for decades with practically no one accepting Christ.' Nevertheless, these are exceptional: 'in most cases, however, the situation is remediable. Arrested growth can be ascribed to faulty procedures'. Thus it becomes a sign of correct procedures and successful ministry if church growth is evident. Conversely, church decline is usually a sign of unsuccessful ministry. The link between success and growth is not absolute but it is the norm: 'sometimes, when a shepherd returns empty-handed, it is because the sheep refuse to be found and flee at his approach. Sometimes, however, empty-handedness becomes a habit and is caused by peering into ravines where there are no sheep, resolutely neglecting those who long to be found in favor of those who refuse to be. Sometimes it is a question of sticking for decades to methods which have proved ineffective.'[23]

By taking numerical growth as the primary aim of mission or outreach, McGavran is fully prepared to accept the functional methods and consequences that follow from this. At several points he uses a market analogy comparing church growth with business development. For example, he argues that 'fog ... prevents intelligent action toward discipling the nations. If Churches and missions deny themselves exact, current, and meaningful accounts of the degree of church multiplication which has – and has not – taken place, how can they take remedial action? The owners of a chain of supermarkets or any other business would think it folly not to know promptly which units are making and which are losing money.'[24] Like the supermarket owner he insists that the churches should indeed learn to distinguish between those situations in which growth is possible and those in which it is not. The latter are then to be by-passed in favour of the former. At another point he insists that 'men use the numerical approach in all worthwhile human endeavour. Industry, commerce, finance, research, government, invention, and a thousand other lines of enterprise derive great profit and much of their stability in development from continual measurement.'[25] Similarly the churches can be regarded as enterprises which can derive profit and stability from continual measurement and action based rigorously upon this measurement.

Again, because numerical growth is primary, McGavran is happy to relegate the contents of church traditions to a secondary role. Despite his own obvious bias in favour of reformed theology he insists that the concept of church growth is relevant to all Christians. He is not at all surprised that 'to denominational theologians church growth looks inadequately theological'. Rather he responds:

> To all such critics we reply, 'The basic positions of church growth are profoundly biblical and theological; but are not a complete theology. Complete *your* theology by building these basic growth concepts as to the urgency and authority of evangelism into it. As you set forth church growth theory and theology for your congregations and your denomination use your own credal statements, your own system. *Voice church growth theology in your patois.* Do not attack church growth as theologically inadequate. Make it adequate according to the doctrines emphasized by your branch of the Church. The test as to whether you have done this or not is whether your congregations are stimulated to vibrant grateful growth such as New Testament churches exemplified.[26]

This is the feature of the theory that Lesslie Newbigin finds most objectionable. As one of the few critical theologians in Britain to subject McGavran to careful scrutiny, he objects on both theological and moral grounds. For Newbigin, reviewing 'the teaching of the New Testament, one would have to say that, on the one hand, there is joy in the rapid growth of the church in its earliest days, but that, on the other hand, there is no evidence that the numerical growth of the church is a matter of primary concern'.[27] He argues that the primary stress in the Pauline epistles is upon quality not quantity, upon faithfulness and integrity of witness not upon numerical growth. For him there is nothing in the New Testament 'comparable to the strident cries of some contemporary evangelists that the salvation of the world depends upon the multiplication of believers.'[28]

Newbigin's most effective objections to the church growth theory are more moral than theological. In a very telling passage he argues:

> In the period following the conversion of Constantine the churches multiplied. So did they at certain times during the conversion of the tribes of northwest Europe, and during the Spanish conquest of Central and South America. We do not look back on these periods with great satisfaction. It might be argued that, for example, the peoples of Central and South America who were baptized by the thousands in the time of the *conquistadors* were not truly converted. But this fails to take account of McGavran's argument that discipling must precede 'perfecting'. On McGavran's principles it is difficult to see how one could fault the procedure of the Spanish and Portuguse missionaries.[29]

Herein lies the dilemma for all theological particularists. If 'salvation' is bestowed exclusively on those who are explicitly Christian, then almost any means must be used to ensure that people become Christian. This was the dilemma facing those involved in the Inquisition and it is the dilemma that still confronts McGavran today. Theological particularism demands extraordinary means. Moral sensitivity is not to the point. It is far more important that individuals are 'saved' than that they are temporarily discomforted. If salvation is effected exclusively through baptism, then enforced baptism may finally be preferable to eternal damnation. If salvation is rather effected only through some verbal acknowledgment of Jesus as Lord, then almost any means must be used to achieve this acknowledgment. If tribal conversion, for example, effectively achieves this end, then it is to be encouraged – as, in fact, McGavran does.

It is clear that McGavran is indeed a theological particularist. In a moment of impatience with critics who see church growth theory as an infringement of 'religious liberty', he argues:

> Behind this facade of sudden sensitivity concerning persuasion, what is really at stake is the truth of the Christian religion. If

there are many paths to God, then for Christians to induce others to follow their path may indeed be self-aggrandizement. But if Christ is the only real Savior, despite all the richness of other faiths in many respects, then persuading men to accept Him is not really open to the charge of selfishness, whatever the imperfections of the human agents of God's love.[30]

On this understanding, the 'imperfections of the human agents' are of very peripheral concern. Numerical growth is the central criterion, because the greater the number the greater the number 'saved'. Agency imperfections are a minor peccadillo. Indeed, McGavran cites with approval the example of Bishop Azariah of Dornakal, who, 'when he first came to the diocese, excommunicated more than six thousand, chiefly for open adultery. Since the Anglicans were taking in thousands, far from stopping growth, his disciplinary action stimulated it. Many of the excommunicated repented and were restored.'[31] The happy result was that church growth was stimulated and former adulterers repented, or at least ceased to be 'open' adulterers. Unfortunately a few others lost their salvific status!

In considering theological responses to church decline the Church Growth Movement provides a systematic account of one extreme. Those constantly attacked by the Movement provide the other. In the 1960s, especially, it was sometimes popular to be disparaging about any attempt to increase church membership. Even those who earned their living from institutional churches in Britain sometimes referred to the objects of such attempts as 'pew fodder'.

There is a strange reluctance amongst some critical theologians to discuss church structures. Whilst remaining fully committed to institutional churches in a private capacity, and whilst being enthusiastic supporters of radical Christian action in public, they seldom articulate in detail the church structures that are necessary to achieve this. In the process, the churches become objects of prophetic judgments, but not of the practical structures that are necessary to respond to these judgments. A very clear example of this is provided recently by Alistair Kee's important book *Domination or Liberation: The Place of Religion in Social Conflict*. The book is challenging and prophetic at many levels. With great skill Kee considers the way churches have acted as agents of gender, race and class domination. He is as fully aware as Paul Badham of the empirical gap between theory and practice within the churches – with the way churches may remain agents of domination even when they appear to be condemning it. He summarizes his findings as follows:

> Religion has historically failed to condemn and oppose domination through discrimination based on gender, race and class. Indeed in quite specific ways religion has legitimized such domination, both protecting it from attack and providing for it the trappings of moral respectability. Religion has assisted in the furthering of domination carried out by others, and has even participated in domination on its own account.[32]

This, however, is not the end of Kee's challenge. He is as committed as I am to praxis and not simply to a theoretical challenge. His repeated criticism of some of those involved, for example, in the feminist movement is that they sometimes imagine that the way to eliminate domination is just to expose it. In contrast he maintains that 'denouncing specific instances of domination will do nothing to end domination; it will only produce alternative forms'. For Kee, domination 'has to be understood as an ideology which hides behind accepted values and respected institutions. While righteous anger is proper as a motive, it provides no critical theory'.[33] Accordingly, he sees hope in the 'ways in which Christianity in the modern world has helped to expose this role, and has begun the transformation by which religion might now actually begin to contribute to liberation in each of these spheres'.[34] In the writings of Leonardo Boff,[35] especially, with his intimate connection between ideology and base communities, Kee sees a way forward for the churches. He argues:

> The church is not guided by theology, by ideas or ideals. Its nature is determined by its mode of religious production. It is therefore not possible to change the nature of the church or relations within it at the level of ideas, for example by exposing and condemning domination. The church and relations within it, can only be changed when the mode of religious production is replaced. And this is precisely what Boff has experienced in the base communities: 'these communities mean a break with the monopoly of social and religious power and the inauguration of a new religious and social process for restructuring both the church

and society, with a different social division of labour as well as an alternative religious division of ecclesiastical labour'. In these communities there is once again a sharing of the religious life. The gifts of the Spirit are not bestowed according to social or religious class. The monopoly is broken and with it the basis of power and consequently the possibility of domination and oppression. The sacramental life is the gift of God to the community and is not the private property of any class.[36]

Yet, having written that, Kee offers the reader no more. The rest of the book is concerned with analysing and criticizing the new religious right in the churches. Perhaps this would not be surprising in one less committed to praxis. But the central critique of *Domination or Liberation* is that gender, race and class forms of domination within Christianity are to be overcome not simply through exposure but through new or renewed religious structures. In the circumstances two pages on these structures is really not sufficient. The detailed discussion of the differing ways that Christians can overcome social constraints and effectively engage in moral and social issues which occupied my previous chapter is absent from Kee. And he gives no consideration at all to the structural considerations necessary for effective deployment and renewal within institutional churches which will occupy my next chapter. McGavran may be right to criticize radical Christians for their general lack of structural specificity.

Further, McGavran does have some justice on his side in claiming that it should not be a matter of complete indifference to churchpeople whether the churches themselves decline or increase. It would be an unusual active supporter of an institution who was completely indifferent to its demise. Even those who suppose that decline is simply inevitable might be tempted sometimes to test this supposition. Of course, McGavran himself would express this far more strongly. His identification of the number of church members with the number of the 'saved' requires him to do so. Yet even if the understanding of faith that I defended in the first chapter – faith viewed primarily as a relationship to God, and, for Christians, a relationship to God in Christ – is adopted, church decline is less than desirable. Without claiming that churches are the sole media of this relationship, churchpeople generally might claim that they are nevertheless important media. And without confusing institutional churches with the kingdom of God, those of us who are members might still believe that they are not unrelated to it. More specifically, we might indeed claim that within corporate worship, and for many of us within the eucharist in particular, our relationship to God in Christ becomes most manifest. If we believe that, then perhaps it ought to be a matter of concern to us that fewer and fewer are themselves party to this worship.

However, a warning is important at this point. Newbigin rightly points out that church increase is not always attained by desirable (especially if one is not a theological particularist) means. It may not even be a primary aim of the New Testament writers. Nor do numerically strong churches always provide the most encouraging models of Christianity. Kee provides a wealth of evidence about the historical role of numerically strong churches in the process of domination. Further, it is arguable that there was far more dissension and unChristian hostility between the numerically strong Victorian churches than there is today between declining British churches. Some sociologists regard ecumenism as an indication of the comparative weakness of institutional churches – since organizations tend to unite when they are weak not when they are strong.[37] Even if ecumenism were simply about organizational unification, this verdict would differ from the theological perception of most of us actively engaged in ecumenical activity. We look back to the bickerings of some of our Victorian predecessors with deep embarrassment and with little inclination to return to this form of ecclesiastical competitiveness. And some of the actions of the mediaeval Universal Catholic Church do not inspire great confidence. Even the usually benign Thomas Aquinas was prepared to support sanctions against the Jews and especially against apostates and 'heretics'.[38] Sociologically it is difficult to avoid the conclusion that universal churches tend to breed their own special form of totalitarianism.

If this warning is heeded church growth cannot be given the centrality that McGavran wishes for it. Nor can the crude link that he makes between successful ministry and the numerical increase of congregations be accepted. Within a general situation of church decline too many clergy are already overburdened with guilt on account of this link. And far too many congregations are happy to burden their clergy with this guilt. It cannot be repeated too often that this link is empirically suspect, theologically contentious, and morally dubious in terms of the methods that it encourages.

Nevertheless, resignation in the face of decline is not the only option for churches. In this limited sense McGavran is surely correct. There are methods and structures that can be learned from the Church Growth Movement which might mollify decline. If the particularist motives which have generated these methods and structures are removed from the theory, and they are then modified accordingly, they might be usable by those of us who would otherwise be antagonistic towards the Movement. The very single-mindedness of McGavran, which at one level makes his work so problematic, at another gives a rigour and concern for structural detail that is often lacking in his critics. It can be difficult at times to penetrate beyond the theological presuppositions that he brings to his work. Further, *Understanding Church Growth* is redolent with repetitions and anecdotes. Even the points that he does make could often have been made by anyone with the use of a little common sense. Nevertheless, a judicious adoption of some of the methods and structures that he proposes in the work might help to edge congregations beyond decline.

Clear membership and population statistics, careful distinctions between different sources and potential sources of membership, and considered and flexible strategies based rigorously upon these statistics and distinctions, are all fundamental to his approach. These three elements are continuously interrelated. He insists that it is important to keep accurate church and general population statistics, but requires at the same time that these statistics must be capable of some use. In other words, they must be functional. It literally serves no purpose to keep disparate statistics which are unrelated to one's future aims. Nor does it serve any purpose to keep statistics which are less than impartial, however distressing they might seem. Careful distinctions are essential in compiling the statistics and it is particularly important to reach objective definitions of church membership if they are to be at all useful for comparing one church situation with another. Careful distinctions are also important if potential sources of new members are to be identified. Finally, it is vital that strategies within churches should be rigorously tailored to the differences involved in specific situations. Strategies must be sufficiently flexible to respond to these differences. Different sources of new membership will require different strategies based rigorously upon the empirical information provided by accurate statistics. Strategies which are time-honoured but not functional are, like disparate statistics or subjective distinctions, to be discarded. Functionality is crucial.

British churches are very adept at compiling statistics and then ignoring them when they deploy their clergy or subsidize specific parishes. In the next chapter I will consider this point at length. The Church of England, for example, has known for many years that the overwhelming majority of the population in England is urban. *Faith in the City* points out that, 'in the century of industrial development from 1831 to 1931 the percentage of the British population living in areas classified as urban rose from thirty four to eighty, and now stands at ninety per cent'.[39] During much of this century an increasing proportion of this urban population has moved into the suburbs. In 1981 the suburban population of Britain was forty-three per cent of the total population.[40] Yet the Church of England continues to deploy a quite disproportionate number of its clergy in rural parishes. Not only that, but it offers these parishes an increasing subsidy at the expense of the urban parishes. McGavran's functional approach would have little difficulty in demonstrating the absurdity of this policy when matched against the ostensive aims of the General Synod to focus upon urban priority areas.

British churches, like churches elsewhere, tend to be ambivalent about the concept of membership. On the one hand most do have electoral rolls, rolls of communicant members, or something similar. They go to some trouble in attempting to keep these rolls up to date and periodically in refining the methods by which they seek to do this. Most also produce openly published statistics as a result of these procedures. In this respect British Roman Catholics are an instructive exception. Their openly published statistics relate only to baptisms and make no distinction between those who are currently active within the church and those who are not. On the other hand most churches are aware that these rolls are relatively fluid and underestimate their support in their community at large. They may also be suspicious of the sectarian tendency to make a sharp distinction between members and non-members and certainly show little enthusiasm for membership exclusion, or excommunication, on either doctrinal or moral grounds. They generally remain tolerant of nominal membership, of civil and folk religion, and of the occasional conformity of large sections of the population. Yet in the process they may become too reluctant to analyse their own membership patterns self-critically. As a result, their membership rolls have little function in identifying possible sources of new, active members.

Few British churches give sustained attention to the differing strategies that might be appropriate for new or renewed members. Because declining churches have a tendency to structural conservatism, they find flexible strategies particularly difficult. It seems safer to stick with existing parish models even when these are manifestly contributing to decline. When church buildings are located away from the local centre of population, when, in a rural situation, they cluster in the charge of a single clergyman and consume most of his or her time, when parish boundaries impede effective pastoral action, when urban laity unrealistically expect their clergy to do all the visiting, it still seems 'safer' to stay with existing structures. Ironically, some churches have shown a degree of flexibility and innovation in their liturgies which they have been much more loathe to show in their parochial structures. Even when they accumulate empirical evidence which demonstrates that these structures are dysfunctional, their response remains inflexible. I have even observed congregations preferring to face extinction rather than make structural changes.

McGavran distinguishes between three different types of membership growth – biological, transfer, and conversion. Biological growth 'derives from those born into Christian families': transfer growth is 'the increase of certain congregations at the expense of others': conversion growth is that 'in which those outside the Church come to rest their faith intelligently on Jesus Christ and are baptized and "added to the Lord" in His Church'.[41] Again it is necessary to remove the particularist presuppositions. 'Christian families' become the families of active churchgoers, and 'those outside the Church ...' become those who are not active churchgoers. This done it becomes clear that there are distinctions to be made here which require different strategies and forms of ministry. It will be evident that encouraging the children of churchgoers themselves to become active within a congregation may be a very different enterprise from encouraging adults who currently have little contact with institutional churches. Further, non-Roman Catholic churches in Britain have surprisingly poor levels of transfer growth – not in the sense of particular congregations increasing at the expense of others (in Britain this is mainly a phenomenon of eclectic city-centre churches), but in the sense of active church-goers who move house becoming active elsewhere. Physical mobility is associated with the loss of active church membership.[42] Amongst major churches in Britain only the Roman Catholic Church experiences little loss of active churchgoers through moving house. Possibly the commitment of the latter is more to 'going to mass' than going to a specific church building. Whatever the reason, every parish minister will know the phenomenon of key office bearers within their own congregation moving away from the area and ceasing to go to church altogether. Encouraging such people to go to a new church may well involve different strategies again.

One of the strongest points of McGavran is that he does alert one to the need to relate flexible strategies to specific goals and situations. In challenging the way declining churches deploy their clergy and use their resources it is essential to specify clear object-ives and then to match these to the most appropriate means. A sociological perspective undoubtedly helps in this enterprise. McGavran himself is more than willing to use sociological tech-niques. Active parochial experience of flexible forms of ministry is also highly relevant. None of these need be the exclusive preroga-tive of conservative evangelicals. Declining churches could change their ways and adopt more flexible and responsive structures. I will argue in the next chapter that, if they have the vision and courage, they are capable of renewal.

5

Structures Beyond Decline

Given the fact that British churches are declining, this book has set out to challenge a number of theological responses to this decline. In the first chapter I argued against a simplistic approach to Christian belief. It is tempting in a situation of decline to blame critical theologians for upsetting the faithful. It is also tempting to try to restore uniformity of belief, presumably in the hope that if Christian faith can be expressed clearly, simply and authoritatively, then people will respond and come back to the churches. In challenging this view I argued that such an approach misunderstands the nature of an increasingly educated society. Pluralism of beliefs is already a feature of most churches, is inescapable in ecumenical theology faculties, and is strongly evident in society at large. Returning to some simplistic uniformity of belief is not the answer for the churches. It might be the answer for exclusive sects which have built barriers against society. But it is not the answer for churches which are still seeking to be a serious part of society.

In the second chapter I argued against a simplistic approach to Christian social action. It is tempting for declining churches to become lobby groups for particular cases. If they can no longer be the central source for moral values in a pluralist society, they could at least espouse specific and admittedly partisan causes. In arguing against this I was very conscious that a more conservative group within declining churches wishes, on the contrary, to stop churches engaging in any moral and social issues and to concentrate instead upon 'the gospel'. Since I accept neither of these positions I spent the third chapter outlining five ways that Christians in a pluralist society can effectively engage in moral and social issues. Taken together these five ways are certainly not simplistic. They place heavy and sometimes competing demands upon Christians. Yet that is what I believe an increasingly educated society demands of us. Attempting to get general assemblies or synods to make high-sounding moral and social judgments is just not sufficient. If we are serious about changing society, then we must think much harder about the effective means that are still open to us to do this. I am sometimes astonished by the naivety of both social activists and apolitical evangelists within the churches.

The fourth chapter set out to challenge simplistic approaches to outreach and evangelism. Declining churches pose a threat to many clergy and congregations. It is only too easy to link 'decline' with 'failure' and 'increase' with 'success'. The Church Growth Movement makes this link particularly crudely and underpins it with an exclusivist, particularist theology. In a situation of depressing decline such theology, and the strategies that are derived from it, offer an obvious temptation to the churches. Once again the hope is raised that churches which distinguish clearly between Christians (members) and non-Christians (non-members) and use a simple gospel message and any means possible to convert the latter, can grow. Growth becomes *the* aim and object of the churches because church growth involves a direct growth in the number of people 'saved'.

However, in arguing against this approach, I am conscious of other Christians within declining churches who seem to object to *any* attempt at Christian outreach. There are others again who simply assume that church decline is an inevitable process and that there is little that anyone can do to reverse or even mollify it. I certainly do not wish to return to any position which links 'increase' with 'success' or which regards 'increase' as the main aim and objective of the churches. Yet I do believe that we ought to be attempting to share our worship with a wider part of society and that we ought to be attempting to draw others into our worshipping communities and congregations. As a parish priest I have always found this inescapable. And as a sociologist I am not convinced that church decline is some ineluctable process and that there are no strategies available to mollify it. Both my academic research and my experience in non-stipendiary parish ministry have convinced me otherwise. Without indulging in the exaggerated claims of the Church Growth Movement, it is possible to suggest ways that churches could seek to counter their current decline. But churches will need to be a good deal more rigorous and self-critical than they appear to be at present if they are to do this.

So, having set out the theological challenges that confront declining churches, this chapter will consider instead structural options which might mollify or even reverse decline. Praxis theology requires theologians not simply to be concerned with ideas but also to give attention to the structures that support, flow from, and even challenge these ideas. If I am convinced that churches should be involved in outreach, then it does become incumbent upon me not just to criticize simplistic evangelism, but to suggest concrete ways in which churches might effectively engage in outreach in a pluralist society. To do this I need to be more rigorous in distinguishing between aims and means and then in suggesting means that are appropriate to these aims.

What aims might be suggested for the churches today in a pluralist society? I have already suggested that Christians should seek more effectively to engage in moral and social action. Yet for most Christians that ought not to be the whole of the churches' action in society. A central function ought also to involve worship and a consequent aim ought to be to engage others in society more deeply in worshipping communities. Without in any way detracting from the importance of moral and social action, in this chapter I will focus upon action which is concerned primarily with worship. Of course there are vital connections between these two aims – social and moral action on the one hand and worship outreach on the other. That is assumed here. Theologians are becoming increasingly sensitive to the interaction between worship, belief and moral and social action. Examples of beliefs and actions being moulded by worship have been suggested (e.g. christology stemming from early Christian prayer direced towards Christ),[1] as have examples of worship being influenced by changing beliefs and actions (e.g. many of the recent liturgical changes). The interrelationship is complex and is not at issue here.[2] However, by focussing upon outreach related to worship, it might be possible to get a clearer vision of a central aim of the churches in society and through this to perceive better the means appropriate to achieve this aim.

For most Christian traditions, worship is primarily a corporate phenomenon. Some types of orthodox Judaism and Islam specify detailed individual and family ritual obligations and limit corporate ritual activity to males. Some types of Hinduism and Buddhism are primarily individualistic in their ritual activity. In contrast, most Christian traditions regard corporate worship as a central undertaking for males and females alike. They may differ in the degree of obligation they place upon their members to attend weekly corporate worship. Roman Catholics and sects tend to insist upon the strictest forms of obligation, whereas national churches regard even some spasmodic attenders as communicant members. Yet most do regard Sunday (or exceptionally Saturday) worship as central. Within eucharistic churches communion is regarded as central to this worship – with churches paradoxically considering it to be so important that either they reserve it for special occasions or they celebrate it as frequently as possible. Frequency of communion is not an accurate guide to its centrality in a particular Christian tradition. It may still be surrounded by interdictions as it is in some traditions that practice only quarterly communion. Further, its comparative frequency in present-day Anglicanism may disguise its importance for past generations of Anglicans who often rose as early as 6 am or 7 am to receive Easter and Christmas communion.

The centrality of corporate worship for most Christian traditions has several important implications when considering their overall aims. Most traditions maintain that it is vital to make adequate provision in terms of buildings, functionaries, and freedom of access to corporate worship. They react most sharply to political regimes that deny them any of these provisions. Historically some have even sought, at times, to impose attendance at corporate worship upon the public at large or to restrict the trading or leisure activities of this public on a Sunday. A few (most remarkably of all in Sweden) have even managed to get the state to pay for church functionaries and/or buildings. However a majority of traditions spend a great deal of their own resources on the provision of buildings and functionaries which they believe are necessary for corporate worship. Indeed, if the centrality of an institution's aims is to be measured by the proportion of its resources that it allocates to them, then, for most Christian traditions, church buildings and functionaries for corporate worship are overwhelmingly important. Many traditions even allow their functionaries very considerable latitude in whatever else they do with their time, provided that they maintain regular corporate worship.

Further, most Christian traditions tend to subordinate private prayer and doctrinal commitment to corporate worship. Space is provided actually within most forms of Christian worship for private prayer and credal affirmation. The individual is invited, or sometimes required, to make silent intercession and confession within corporate worship and then to make a verbal credal affirmation. The latter is particularly strange. Credal affirmation is not obviously prayer and its stylized, corporate and archaic form ensures that it is not exactly a personal affirmation of faith. Despite its initial appearance, as a ritual activity it may have as much to do with corporate identity as it does with individual belief (as a result 'we believe ...' may well be more accurate than 'I believe'). This becomes even more evident in the congregational hymn that plays so important a role in reformed forms of worship and, today, even within many Roman Catholic forms of family mass. The purely cognitive elements of the hymn can soon be subordinated to the music and corporate singing. Modern congregations can, as a result, cheerfully sing hymns in immediate proximity fashioned initially for competing Christian traditions. They can even sing repeatedly a hymn such as William Blake's *Jerusalem* with little understanding of the central symbolism that he used. For many the hymn is less an expression of private faith than a powerful medium of religious identity, as its pivotal role in religious television clearly demonstrates.

Finally corporate worship often provides an important element in denominational identity. For example, within Anglicanism there has, from its inception, typically been considerable latitude in doctrinal interpretation. Neither has Anglicanism been characterized by rigid central control. Within England at least (although not always in parts of the Third World) Anglican bishops have been carefully controlled in the power they have over their own dioceses. Yet, until very recently, Anglicans have had a common prayer book and thus a common identity.[3] Within Roman Catholicism the latin mass provided an even more potent medium of identity, since this was not even subject to the variables introduced by differing languages. In both churches it is hardly surprising that liturgical change generates such strong feelings. Liturgical experiment inevitably introduces a change of identity: numerous alternative forms, especially when combined with the vernacular, serve to change this identity further. As a response to modern pluralism I am convinced that these changes are thoroughly appropriate.

Nevertheless, critics of liturgical change are correct to point to the link between liturgy and identity.[4]

Even reformed churches which avoid a written liturgy still have forms of corporate worship which are directly relevant to identity. They too are subject to internal disputes about what forms are thought to be appropriate. The hymn book can sometimes take the place of the prayer book as the bone of contention between traditionalists and radicals. Changing the hymn book or introducing modern hymns from outside the hymn book can act as a medium of identity change. Changing the ritual process surrounding the reception of communion – for example, from individual cups to a common cup, or from elders distributing the bread and wine to the people coming to the table to receive – is also a particularly potent way of changing identity. The reformers themselves were well aware of the symbolic importance of key features of corporate worship – the position of the pulpit, the public display of the Bible, the dress and deportment of the minister, the corporate responses and singing of the congregation, the space between minister and congregation. The variations possible between these features and many other physical features of corporate worship act as important means of differentiation, and thus of separate identity, between apparently similar reformed traditions.

If the provision of corporate worship is regarded as a central (but not, of course, the only) aim of British churches, what means are required to implement this aim today? Britain abounds with church buildings, the Church of England alone provides a stipendiary clergyman on average for every five thousand people in the population, and freedom of access to worship is guaranteed by the state. Every city and most towns offer a wide variety of Christian traditions of corporate worship and within city centres, in particular, eclectic congregations can be found representing extremes of churchmanship within a variety of denominations. For the mobile, especially, Britain offers potential worshippers a bewildering array of choices. Yet churchgoing is a declining phenomenon and fewer and fewer avail themselves of the choices that are readily available to them. The reason for this situation seems to lie more with the population at large than with the churches. The latter provide more than adequate means to meet their aim of providing corporate worship. It is the population that ignores these means.

This claim misses crucial discrepancies between the aims and means of present-day churches. The parochial system of the Church of England and the Church of Scotland was designed to meet the needs of an overwhelmingly rural population. In this situation it was considered to be important to provide church buildings and full-time clergy for every parish in Britain. In parts of Britain this was never fully achieved until the middle of the nineteenth century.[5] For example, in my own village in the Borders no vicarage was provided for almost three hundred years until 1836 and, not unexpectedly, the vicar was non-resident for much of the eighteenth century. In 1758 'in Lent the children were "called upon to be catechised, but never any appear", which was not surprising as the inhabitants were "all of the Presbyterian Persuasion, one family only excepted", and the glory of that one family was somewhat dimmed from the parson's point of view, as half of its members were Roman Catholics. Of other ministrations there were none. "The Holy Sacrament has never been administered here since I knew it, because there is not a congregation."'[6] Yet ironically the provision of a resident full-time clergyman took place at the very time that the rural population of Britain started moving to industrial cities looking for work. Today the village population is only a fifth of the size of its Victorian population and ninety per cent of the British population as a whole is urban, not rural. Yet the Church of England still deploys half of its stipendiary clergy in rural and small town situations.

This discrepancy is considerably compounded by economic factors. If aims and means are to be related one might expect an institution like the Church of England, with its very considerable financial means, to use these means to further its aims. Up to a point it does this. By far the greatest part of its usable income is spent on clergy stipends. Further, since the discrepancies between clerical stipends were highlighted twenty years ago in the Paul Report,[7] there has been a sustained attempt (assisted very considerably by rapid inflation) to equalize these stipends. If in my grandfather and great-grandfather's days middle-class clerical poverty in their parishes was tolerated alongside considerable clerical affluence in otherwise similar neighbouring parishes, today this is seldom the case. Most clergy receive a very similar stipend, whether they are in urban or rural or once affluent or more impoverished charges. Yet the effect of this commendable egalitarianism, when combined with disaproportionate rural deployment, has been to divert urban finances into rural situations. It is not simply that the income from inherited wealth (largely through the Church Commissioners) is used disproportionately on rural stipends. That in itself would be a sufficiently serious indication of a discrepancy between aims and means. Rather, income that is generated through quotas in wealthy urban parishes is being used actually to supplement rural stipends. In the deanery I have just left the rural charges with full-time stipendiary priests pay diocesan quotas which represent, at best, a third of the cost of maintaining their priests.

In terms of McGavran functionalism, a church that does this simply cannot be serious in its aims. Twelve years of working as a non-stipendiary rural parish priest and observing diocesan deployment have convinced me that there is a very serious gap between aims and means. Once again there is a gulf between theory and practice, between the claims that institutional churches make and their actual practices. This work and observation have convinced me that present patterns of deployment are not just misguided but actually contribute directly to decline.

Perhaps I should make it clear immediately that what follows is not intended as a direct criticism of the hierarchy in the Newcastle diocese. That would be very unfair. I must be specific because the task of formulating new structures is otherwise soon lost in generalities. And in any case it has been tested by my own very specific parish experience. Yet what I say of course applies more generally to other dioceses. The Newcastle diocese is not unique: it was simply my own situation. Further the hierarchy of any diocese are inevitably caught up in the compromises and vested interests that surround them. Time and again when I challenged particular appointments I was told that I did not really appreciate the personnel problems involved. It *is* very difficult successfully to challenge established patterns in conservative institutions – especially ones that already feel threatened by long-term decline. And it is surely even more difficult for individuals to do this if they are subject to personnel pressures within the time constraints of modern church bureaucracy.

Yet I am convinced that established patterns do need to be challenged. The temptation for declining churches is to stick to what is already established rather than to embark upon risky change. Liturgical changes may act as something of a warning. If once it was hoped that they would encourage an increase in churchgoing – since they would release churches from archaic forms and make them more relevant to the modern world – this does not seem to have happened. In Europe as a whole liturgical change in the Roman Catholic Church and in Britain in the Anglican Church has been accompanied by an accelerated decline in churchgoing.[8] Even if these two are unconnected, they do not at first sight support the view that change can mollify decline (although it is still possible that liturgical renewal has saved a bad situation from becoming even worse). However, this warning misses the point. In the instance of deployment there is empirical evidence that current patterns are actually contributing to decline – *even within the rural situation.*

This can be demonstrated quite simply. Twelve years ago when I first came to North Northumberland there were six full-time stipendiary clergy in the rural part of the deanery and four in Berwick-upon-Tweed. The total population of the deanery was less than 17,000, with four-fifths of this population living in Berwick-upon-Tweed. Twenty years before I arrived there were another four rural clergy and one additional one in the town. Today there are four rural clergy and just three in the town (one of whom now looks after a rural church in addition). The balance between rural and urban clergy in the deanery is clearly shifting. Yet after thirty years four out of seven clergy are still responsible for a mere one-fifth of the population of the deanery. This imbalance remains both because of continued appointments of full-time clergy to rural charges of less than one thousand people and because the number of town clergy has also been reduced.

In the diocese as a whole the imbalance is even more disastrous. The Newcastle diocese combines very considerable urban deprivation in Newcastle-upon-Tyne itself with, in Northumberland, one of the most thinly spread rural populations in England. This difficult combination serves to mask the degree of imbalance in deployment that it contains. It is, though, an imbalance which depicts in microcosm the Church of England as a whole. In *Faith in the City*[9] the Newcastle diocese, as a result, is only listed twenty-first (out of forty-three) in terms of its ratio of population to parochial clergy. So if Birmingham (with 7,094 people per clergy) and Hereford (with 2,023) are taken as the two poles, Newcastle appears to sit somewhere in the middle (with 4,715). In reality the situation is far worse than that in the most populous parts of the diocese. There are still parishes in Newcastle-upon-Tyne of some

30,000, 'looked after' by a clergyman single-handed. Simultaneously there are rural charges of less than 1,000. If all the full-time parochial clergy are added together, out of 186 (in 1986)[10] only 90 work specifically in Newcastle-upon-Tyne, in which, of course, the vast majority of the local population lives. Of the remaining 96 parochial clergy not all have tiny rural charges: some serve in towns like Berwick-upon-Tweed. Yet even these are serving only a fraction of the population in the whole area covered by the diocese. The bulk of the urban population is effectively without Anglican clergy. It can have little effective contact with such a thinly spread parochial clergy who, in turn, can find little time to do anything other than hurried rites of passage. This is a pattern of urban ministry extremely well situated to decline.

Ironically it is also a pattern well suited to decline in the rural part of the diocese. As can be seen from the pattern in North Northumberland – and even more dramatically in rural areas, such as Norfolk or Southern Kent, which have numerous historic church buildings – the number of full-time rural clergy is slowly being reduced. The dominant model for achieving this is parish amalgamation: single-handed rural clergy become responsible for an increasing number of tiny parishes and church-buildings. There is nothing particularly new about the amalgamation model. It was a strong feature of the eighteenth century in North Northumberland. Yet its consequences are known. Increasing amalgamation leads to decline. It manifestly did in the eighteenth century and the careful research of Leslie Francis suggests that it still does so today. Using the sophisticated statistical technique of 'path analysis' in his survey of rural congregations in Norfolk, Francis comes to the following critical observation:

> After differences in population have been taken into account, the number of parishes in a benefice makes no difference at all to the number of names on the electoral roll, but it does make a real difference to the number of people who come into contact with the church on a typical Sunday. If a single parish benefice and a multi-parish benefice of the same population figures are compared, we would expect the combined electoral roll figures of the multi-parish benefice to be roughly the same as the electoral roll figures of the single parish benefice. However we would still expect fewer people to attend church on a Sunday in the multi-

parish benefice. This means that, if two clergymen have responsibility for the same number of parishioners, the one who has
three churches to look after rather than one will have just as
many nominal churchgoers on his electoral roll, but significantly
less active churchgoers in his congregation.[11]

From this Francis draws three conclusions. Firstly that 'three
small churches cut less ice than one large church'. Secondly that it
is difficult for clergy with three small churches 'to keep the active
commitment of the potential church members'. And thirdly that
such clergy 'are likely to feel that their pastoral contact is less
rewarding and less successful than their colleagues working among
a similar number of people in a single parish benefice'.[12] The
amalgamation model leads both to churchgoing decline and eventually to clergy dissatisfaction. Those who have observed rural
ministry at first-hand will be well aware of the latter. Multi-charge
rural ministry can be extremely depressing.

I discovered the ultimate horror story on a sabbatical in Zambia
in 1980. There the chronic shortage of full-time, trained clergy
affects most denominations, including the Roman Catholics. As a
result, most rural congregations are led for much of the year by
laypeople with little or no training and expect a visit from their
minister or priest only on rare occasions. One United Church
minister I met was 'looking after' 150 different congregations on
this basis. Several consequences emerged from this pattern of
ministry. The full-time clergy were generally assured of a rapturous
reception on their spasmodic visits (in Britain it is laypeople who
are the spasmodic visitors to church!). I was even greeted rapturously
when the congregation had really expected the bishop. It was, of
course, very difficult for the clergy themselves to have any serious
knowledge of the specific needs of the individual congregations in
their charge. On the other hand, congregations across denominations devised their own folk services, which sometimes owed little
to their sponsoring denomination. The high attendances characteristic of the rare clergy visits did not persist meantime and the
dominant interim services were the object of considerable local
dissension.

The amalgamation model is increasingly a feature of a number of
British churches. Rural Methodism has almost been destroyed by
it in some areas and the United Reformed Church seems to be

following suit. Even Roman Catholicism in rural Britain has opted for the model. The Church of Scotland, with its national network of carefully defined parishes, provides a prime example. The fact that it has been much more ruthless than the Church of England in its policy of amalgamation (partly because the Union of 1929 left it with duplicate church buildings in many parts of Scotland), means that many rural ministers have sole responsibility for five or more parishes extending over a very wide area. At the same time, it has also been more ruthless than the Church of England in making church buildings redundant that are deemed to be superfluous. A prime factor in this situation is that none of these British churches has the inherited wealth of the Church of England. As a result none can afford to deploy full-time stipendiary clergy into charges that raise only a third of their cost. They are all subject to much stricter financial constraints. Similarly the Scottish Episcopal church, enjoying little of the wealth of its sister church, has been forced to deploy most stipendiary clergy into charges which are financially capable of supporting them. Yet to do this in rural areas, most churches which continue to have a rural role opt for the amalgamation model. Clustering a group of churches under a single stipendiary minister or priest provides a viable economic basis. Unfortunately it also provides for rural decline and clerical depression.

The present disastrous situation is caused by a number of factors. Stipendiary rural ministry depended for its support in the past upon there being a sufficiently large rural population in Britain, upon ministers who were prepared to accept varying amounts of remuneration, and, in the national churches, upon a system of enforced rural tithes and/or endowments. Not one of these three factors pertains today. The population of Britain is now overwhelmingly urban. Clergy expect to receive equitable remuneration, even when their workload varies enormously. And the much resented tithing system was abolished in my grandfather's days (to his great relief) and, more recently, inflation has reduced to insignificance most rural endowments. Given these drastic changes, a stipendiary rural ministry can only be maintained in most churches by increasing amalgamation. The Church of England alone can mollify this process somewhat by diverting much needed urban funds into rural parishes – thus perpetuating an anachronistic situation which contributes to both urban and rural decline.

How have the British churches allowed this to happen? I can only imagine that they have failed to give adequate attention to aims and means. If they asked themselves rigorously what their aims are and whether or not present rural deployment is meeting these aims, they would surely realize how inappropriate the present structures are. They might also spot a clue about alternative structures. They might see the obvious dangers inherent within the amalgamation model *for the rural situation itself*. They might also see that it is ill-judged to deploy so many stipendiary clergy (even when they can still just afford to do so) in rural areas when the general population of Britain is overwhelmingly urban. Further, they might see that the Church of England is making a bad situation even worse by indirectly contributing to urban decline as well. The present policy of the Church of England does not simply exacerbate rural decline (through increasing amalgamation), it actually serves to divert funds which could have been used to deploy more clergy in needy urban situations.

Why don't urban clergy in the Church of England try to change this disastrous policy? For twelve years in the Newcastle diocese I found myself increasingly baffled by this question. I could see why the rural clergy did not wish to see changes. The contrast between rural Northumberland and the urban decay of parts of Tynemouth made this obvious. Even the growing depression caused by rural amalgamation seldom outweighed this contrast. Nor did the difficulties created for those with active minds in actually filling the day when surrounded by a rural population which is as busily occupied as others are in twentieth century Britain. Even my presence as a neighbouring priest-in-charge of a parish little different in size from their own did not provoke them to seek changes. Yet this was despite the fact that I and two others in the diocese were doing this whilst having full-time jobs elsewhere. But why not the urban clergy?

I should have known. Their comparative silence had a perfectly obvious social explanation. The clergy of the Church of England exist in fairly isolated enclaves. Synodical government has para-doxically contributed further to this isolation. If, once, most parochial clergy met periodically at diocesan assemblies, today they may never meet. A significant group never stands for election to diocesan synods and another group never fails to stand. Diocesan synods have, as a result, become enclaves of professional élites, whilst other and perhaps more numerous, enclaves have little or no contact with those outside their local deanery. The professional élites who now dominate diocesan synods are particularly attractive to those with some axe to grind – whether it is the blocking of the ordination of women or the preservation of rural deployment. Further, their single-mindedness and active experience tend to preclude others without this experience from challenging their views. It is the professional élites amongst both rural and urban clergy who tend to meet today. The bulk of the rural and urban clergy seldom if ever meet.

Not surprisingly, this places a great deal of authority upon those rural clergy who are members of a diocesan pastoral committee. When I asked individuals from urban parishes who were on this committee why they supported present patterns of deployment, they always expressed ignorance. They explained that, when particular rural charges became vacant, they simply did not have the local knowledge to challenge those who came from that area. Because over half of the parochial clergy were already deployed outside Newcastle-upon-Tyne (and perhaps because they were also relatively free from other commitments), they were well represented on the committee. A professional élite soon becomes a self-perpetuating élite.

The effect of these social factors is to create a church which is a long way away from the local, outward-looking and participating church envisaged by the authors of *Faith in the City*. The picture of multiple urban deprivation that they present is manifest in parts of Newcastle-upon-Tyne. Sadly the picture of the Church of England failing to respond adequately to the urban deprived is also a feature of the Newcastle diocese. Despite the past contribution and 'faithful presence' of the Church of England in urban priority areas (UPAs), the authors argue that 'unless there is considerable reform this contribution will be progressively weakened, and in places the survival of the Church itself may be threatened.[13] They believe that there is a real need for urgency in the present situation of growing urban multiple deprivation:

> If the Church of England as an institution is committed to staying and growing in UPAs, then much of our evidence suggests that it will have to change. It is faced not only with the general decline of organized Christianity in England but also with the particular pressures associated with the UPAs themselves. The

growing crisis in our UPAs is reflected in the life of the Church within them. It can be seen in the lack of local leadership, the never-ending struggles with money and buildings, and the power-lessness associated with being divorced from the centres of power. And there is the fact, as we have already stressed, that historically the Church of England had failed to reach or to keep the urban working-classes. Submission upon submission to us has said that the Church of England's organization and ministry have been so completely middle-class that working-class expressions of reli-gion have not been encouraged.[14]

The report might have added the Church of England's organiza-tion and ministry has been so disproportionately rural – even in some dioceses containing UPAs – that urban working-class expres-sions of religion have not been encouraged. In this respect the Church of England is more culpable than most other British churches, since it alone has the resources for effective action in UPAs. Understanding the social factors which have led it to divert these resources into rural parishes could act as a necessary spur to effective reform.

What can be done to produce effective reform? *Faith in the City* provides many important suggestions for new structures of urban ministry. Given its remit, it naturally pays no attention to rural ministry. However, my argument has been that the two are in-extricably linked. A church's pattern of rural deployment has direct implications for its pattern of urban deployment. For this reason I will make suggestions about rural deployment before examining the detailed urban suggestions of *Faith in the City*.

My criticisms of the amalgamation model have already contained a clue about possible alternatives. The churches' commitment to paying a full and equitable stipend to those engaged in rural ministry is the source of the problem. The rural situation which might have supported this undertaking has disappeared beyond foreseeable recall. The general population is now overwhelmingly urban and the privileged means of supporting rural stipends (from enforced tithes, rural endowments, or the private means of the clergy themselves) are unlikely to return. The model is exhausted and an attempt to keep it going will cost the churches too dear. If the churches are to maintain a trained ministry in the countryside, it will need to be largely unpaid.

Of course some would immediately question this conditional clause. I am very aware that not all accept the need for a trained ministry. They argue that house-churches, worshipping communities, base-communities, or whatever, can function very well without a trained ministry. They sometimes point to earliest Christianity as a precedent for this and see clericalization as a regressive phase of church 'development'. I accept a part of this argument. Yet I am also aware of the social dangers that have faced religious organizations attempting to manage without a trained ministry. Few have succeeded in this. Most develop at the very least a form of 'lay' leadership which looks suspiciously like the professional ministry of other religious organizations. Sociologically, trained leadership is important for the identity, control, maintenance and directionality of most social institutions. And those British churches which have attempted to sustain their rural congregations through a predominantly lay leadership – the obvious example is the Methodists – do not provide encouragement for this more radical position. I am convinced by those who argue that effective rural ministry should contain a balance of both 'professional' clergy and others who have trained specifically for non-stipendiary ministry.[15]

But from where are churches to find a predominantly unpaid trained ministry? Clergy frequently ask me this question, even when they realize that I have had non-stipendiary charges in the Edinburgh and Newcastle dioceses for the last fifteen years. On more than one occasion my local deanery synod solemnly discussed non-stipendiary ministry, expressing grave doubts about whether anyone in full employment would have sufficient time for rural ministry, even while I was sitting there. Let me suggest five obvious sources for this form of ministry.

Firstly, there are the stipendiary extra-parochial clergy to be found in most churches, but present in every diocese in the Church of England. It has always been essential to me as priest to function as a priest in a specific worshipping congregation. I have always been puzzled by colleagues who are content to return to the pew or to play a very subsidiary role from one Sunday to the next. Conducting regular worship, preaching, celebrating the sacrament, and being the pastor to others in and beyond the congregation, were amongst the main reasons for offering myself for ordination. From what I gather from most of my students who are ordinands, they too have very similar reasons. Yet most dioceses assume that some of their most senior clergy should function otherwise. Ironically, during my twelve years in the Newcastle diocese a senior post actually became extra parochial. Whilst several of us with very busy and responsible jobs found time for parochial work, others within the diocese were fully stipendiary but extra-parochial.

Further, most of the clergy teaching in theological colleges and, paradoxically, some teaching full-time on non-stipendiary ministry training courses, are extra-parochial. Yet I am convinced that nearly all of us would be more fulfilled as priests or ministers if we had charge of a congregation. It could be a crucial testing ground of our ministry and a way of earthing what we do or say or teach in the realities of a worshipping community. Again this is praxis theology. If accepted, perhaps we could come to expect all stipendiary clergy also to be parochial clergy (cathedrals counting for just one parish). The supposition that church committees of one sort or another should take precedence over this has always seemed to me to be misplaced. If parishes came first, rural parishes might well be filled by those, however senior, with additional extra-parochial duties. Why not bishops as well?

Secondly, there are previously trained clergy in many churches who are employed outside the churches. For one reason or another, we trained and often functioned for a while as stipendiary clergy, but then chose to take outside employment. Undoubtedly many do this because they found that they came to dislike parochial ministry. However, this is certainly not true for all of us. My own 'outside employment' would traditionally not have been considered to be 'outside' at all, and I never actually left parochial ministry, only stipendiary parochial ministry. Yet I have discovered the joys of being a country priest whilst simultaneously enjoying my university career. I believe that others could be encouraged to do this. Many churches and some dioceses have as yet been reluctant to let such clergy have full charge of a rural congregation. In this respect the Newcastle diocese has been very progressive. Despite the misgivings of some, it is now clear that it does work. Parishes are generally pleased to have their own clergyman, even as a commuter, rather than share a clergyman with a collection of other parishes. In many rural areas they may also get someone rather younger and more energetic than they might otherwise have done.

Of course such clergy need to be efficient. If their time is limited it needs to be used effectively and the ministry of the rest of the congregation needs to be mobilized. For me one of the most important discoveries of non-stipendiary ministry has been that it can make the 'priesthood of all believers' a reality in ways that are just a theoretical construct in other situations. For stipendiary rural clergy to insist that the laity must do some priestly functions – when the laity itself knows that such clergy are not in fact overburdened – may be less than realistic. For non-stipendiary clergy, who have the same time constraints as their congregations, this becomes a necessity. So, when £20,000 was needed to re-roof the parish church, the laity took total charge of the fund-raising. I continued with more priestly roles and did not even sit on the fund-raising committee. And, of course, the members raised the money far more effectively, quickly and enthusiastically than I could ever have done (especially for a church roof). By that stage they had learned some of the deeper implications of non-stipendiary ministry.

Thirdly, there are those trained especially for non-stipendiary ministry. Slowly churches are beginning to realize the importance of this group, although they seldom as yet give them charge over parishes. A few churches, such as my own now, the Scottish Episcopal Church, have, for financial reasons, known their importance for longer. Parts of this church would hardly function at all but for the dedication of a large number of non-stipendiary ministers. As a phenomenon relatively new to British churches it naturally causes some perplexity. Clergy have frequently voiced to me doubts about the quality of training for non-stipendiary ministry. My experience of teaching on several courses, and examining the ethics papers from throughout the country, does not confirm these doubts. Some of the very best (and, I am afraid, worst) ethics papers that I have seen have come from non-stipendiary training courses rather than from full-time theological colleges. The standard of some of those coming forward from these courses is extremely high. They are often highly intelligent and well-organized people who have additional energy to give to the ministry. The fact that these courses recruit a high level of graduates and professionals does mean that they are predominantly middle-class.[16] I am afraid that *Faith in the City* is probably wrong to imagine that this could be an important source of local, working-class priests or ministers.[17] But what it does mean is that stipendiary clergy express academic doubts about this group at their peril. Many are already very able academically and the non-stipendiary courses provided generally by the Church of England, the United Reformed Church, and the Church of Scotland, are to my knowledge based upon serious, critical theology. Only the Scottish Episcopal Church has as yet by-passed such theology in some of its non-stipendiary courses.

Of course not all of the clergy in these three groups will be able to minister to rural charges. Many of those in the second and third groups will need to remain in urban areas because of their paid employment. Not all of those in secular employment will be able or even willing to commute on a daily basis. Nevertheless, having done exactly that for twelve years, I know that it does work. In theory it sounds ludicrous to teach full-time in Edinburgh, yet commute daily from a rural parish in the Scottish Borders. Yet in practice it does work. For those who cannot commute there is still vital work to be done, especially in UPAs. However, for those who can, there is a more pressing task – ministering to rural parishes in order to release their stipendiary clergy to work in urban areas where a majority of the population now lives.

My experience has taught me that many assume too readily that effective parochial ministry is incompatible with regular commuting. Commuters themselves often know otherwise. Many on the rural edges of London, Birmingham or Manchester will already know that they can be active within their local communities even if they are absent during the daytime for five days in the week. What they soon discover is that so are most of their neighbours, whether or not they actually commute. It is frequently supposed that stipendiary rural ministers can be fully occupied visiting their parishioners in the daytime during the week. If they are frank such ministers know that this is seldom the case. It is difficult to find even the elderly at home in the countryside in daylight, let alone the young. Clergy commuting to secular employment or to a central diocesan job, may actually identify more closely with the present-day life-styles of their parishioners than do their stipendiary rural colleagues.

Again, new work patterns may make rural ministry more attractive for some in secular employment. The advent of computers and modern communication systems allows an increasing section of the population to work from home. If once some financial and business jobs could only be carried out in urban settings, today this is fast changing. It is already possible to envisage a situation in which some rural clergy will work from home to support themselves financially, whilst living in the community that forms their ministry.

One of the ironies facing clergy in the third group is that it is often the parishes that least require a non-stipendiary ministry that in practice produce the most non-stipendiary ministers. Within the Scottish Episcopal Church, which has perhaps the most extensive experience of any church of training people for this form of ministry, some affluent urban congregations now have four or five non-stipendiary priests serving alongside a full-time stipendiary priest. In such a situation it becomes all the more important to encourage these non-stipendiary priests to be more adventurous in their forms of ministry. If they can be encouraged to venture out into the countryside, they can be most effectively deployed. If not, they can be challenged to serve the less affluent in an urban setting. In either instance, I am convinced that they would be more fulfilled in their ministry and more effectively used by their church than at present.

A very simple principle is at work here – those who are ordained should use their time as effectively as possible. The time that the clergy in these three groups can give to parochial ministry is strictly limited. So, if they are to have an effective parochial ministry, it needs to be carefully defined and limited. In contrast, stipendiary parochial clergy are given a stipend to allow them to work full-time in their parishes. So, if they are also to have an effective parochial ministry, it should be in parishes where the need is greatest. Since the population of Britain is now so overwhelmingly urban, it is the urban parishes which have the greatest need. Rural charges are no longer appropriate for full-time stipendiary clergy. However, they are highly appropriate for those clergy with strictly limited time for parochial ministry who are able to commute or to work from their rural homes. If rural ministry is impossible for individuals within these three groups, then it is important that they should be offered a challenging urban ministry which is also carefully defined and limited. Once traditional urban parish structures and boundaries are questioned, this too becomes possible.

Fourthly, there are retired or semi-retired clergy. The Scottish Episcopal Church has made extensive use of this group of clergy to staff some of its smaller rural churches. Parishes openly advertise in the *Church Times* offering retired clergy a house, expenses, and usually a delightful setting, in return for a parochial ministry. It may be difficult permanently to manage a particular church on this basis. Leslie Francis provides clear evidence that clergy over sixty years old tend to attract a diminishing and increasingly elderly congregation.[18] This, like the amalgamation model, may be a long-term recipe for decline. Yet for a while, and when mixed with other patterns of ministry, or even when supported by a neighbouring parish, it can be an important way of ensuring that rural congregations do have their own trained ministry. It is even possible to envisage a well-organized church or diocese that offered urban clergy, once past the age of sixty, the option of a limited rural ministry. For many clergy the prospect of a rural ministry is very attractive. From first-hand experience I can vouch for this attraction. I look back over the last twelve years with a sense of privilege and pleasure. Yet some bishops imagine from this that it is right to place clergy who are still in their forties or fifties in rural parishes to 'give them country experience'. I still find this quite astonishing. The idea that someone with energy and comparative youth should expend this full-time on a small rural parish, when the needs elsewhere are so great, is truly amazing.

Fifthly, there might even be a group of partly-paid clergy. All the other options have worked on the assumption that clergy should be paid equitably but that resources should no longer be diverted into rural parishes to provide equitable stipends there. But supposing clergy wish to have a rural ministry and yet are prepared to finance this partly themselves. Naturally it would be better, if they are still comparatively young and energetic, that they should minister in an urban setting. Yet, if they are determined to exercise a rural ministry and are prepared to make this an experimental ministry, perhaps churches should rethink their policies on remuneration. Of course, this remuneration must come from within the rural parish itself: it is vital not to divert funds which could be better spent on urban ministry. With this proviso, why not?

This is not a plea for some return to the old days of grossly unequal stipends, but rather a plea for greater flexibility. A stipend is not a reward but rather a means of releasing someone to give all of their time to ministry. Where such ministry is needed full-time it serves a real purpose. But it has become increasingly clear to me that, by late twentieth-century standards, rural ministry is only a part-time occupation. Amalgamation can cause clergy considerable difficulties on a Sunday. However, for the rest of the week rural clergy can be very seriously under-occupied. Compared with the standards of time-keeping and productivity expected in other professions, rural clergy often continue to be relatively leisured. As a result, jobs such as preparing magazine copy, writing sermons, or visiting those in hospital, can each occupy the best part of a day. A non-stipendiary priest with a full-time outside job, in contrast, of necessity must devote a fraction of the time to such tasks. For the latter, overlapping functions and meticulous use of time are prerequisites. In a bygone age a relatively leisured clergy doubtless performed a variety of important functions in society (in literature, poetry, science, philosophy, etc.). In an age of specialists the country parson is fortunate to have even a theological work accepted for publication. Perhaps the more enterprising really could explore the possibility of combining a partly-paid rural ministry with other forms of remuneration.

A few churches are already open to this form of ministry. However, as women come to exercise a more central role in ministry, so all chuches will need to become considerably more open in this respect. Currently, amongst women doctors, there is extensive discussion of the need of many married women to balance their professional duties with motherhood. Many will be only too aware of the dilemma expressed recently by a woman GP: 'every working mother struggles against the incompatible demands made by job and family. An insufficient input into either sphere lessens the satisfaction intrinsic in this dual lifestyle.'[19] If once it was assumed that women should simply choose between the two (especially in the churches), today this is increasingly questioned. Instead, many general practices are discovering the gifts that a woman doctor, even working less than full-time, can bring. Churches too could make a similar discovery.

All five patterns of rural ministry are open to churches if they can learn to be more flexible. If aims and means are to be seriously related in the present situation, then flexible means are essential. From my own experience I know that they work. In attempting to assess my own twelve years of rural ministry as rigorously as possible, I could find little evidence that it contributed to decline. In terms of communicants, confirmands, new members, discussion groups, liturgical renewal, lay initiative, participation from the local school and sometimes a Sunday school, the parish seemed to be active. Observing others in a similar role, parishes generally responded well and showed few of the signs of decline typical of amalgamated parishes. I have now started a ministry in my third non-stipendiary charge. Again I am convinced that it can work.

Congregations do respond to energy, enthusiasm, liveliness, thoughtful planning, and attractive worship. Non-stipendiary clergy can provide these qualities just as well as stipendiary clergy. I have become convinced that for congregations the stipend, or even full-timeness, is of secondary importance. If rural congregations are to edge beyond decline these other qualities are far more significant. A renewed rural ministry could offer them if churches have sufficient courage and flexibility.

Courage and flexibility will also be needed if churches are to renew their urban ministry. By shifting rural ministry away from a stipendiary basis, churches should be able to deploy many more clergy into the urban situation where they are most required. The array of new structures suggested by *Faith in the City* provides a blueprint of how this could be done. Amongst the report's key suggestions are; clergy selection, training, deployment and support, parish boundaries, use of church buildings, ecumenical co-operation, lay training and participation, and financial assistance by wealthier parishes. Amongst the clergy interviewed, the report found that fifty-nine per cent of UPA clergy 'saw their parishes as inadequately staffed',[20] whereas only thirty-one per cent of other clergy felt the same, and that thirty-six per cent of the UPA clergy (compared with fifteen per cent of the other clergy) felt 'exhuastion'. The UPA clergy experienced problems at many levels: like their parishioners they experienced high levels of burglaries, acts of violence and abuse, inadequate physical provisions and support by colleagues, and considerable schooling difficulties. In arguing for improved training and support from the wider body of the churches, the authors were conscious of the need to deploy more highly moti-vated clergy into UPAs. There is also a desperate need in many UPAs to select, train and deploy more black clergy (if necessary by positive discrimination).

The authors of *Faith in the City* argued that it is essential that churches in UPAs become neighbourhood churches:

The importance of neighbourhoods suggests that consideration should be given to:
(1) the need to revise parochial boundaries to relate more closely to such neighbourhoods (as is already possible under the Pastoral Measure);
(2) the development of small neighbourhood-based worship centres. This could lead to 'multi-centre' or 'multi-cellular'

strategies for the local church, reflecting a commitment to a
locality and not simply to a congregation;
(3) the development of centres, preferably ecumenical, in each
neighbourhood (for example in house groups) which reach out in
care and concern for the whole life of the neighbourhood and all
its people. Small groups for prayer, Bible study, healing, and
theological reflection on local issues would be based on them.[21]

The language and theological presuppositions are very different
from McGavran. Yet the urban strategy is very similar. The authors
of *Faith in the City* are clear about their aims and of the need for
radical and flexible means to achieve these aims in UPAs. Whereas
McGavran writes about 'planting churches' in highly populated
urban areas, they write instead about developing 'neighbourhood-
based worship centres'. Liberation theologians, in turn, tend to
write about 'base communities'. For all, it is essential that these
worshipping communities (my own term) should be developed
from local communities upwards, rather than imposed on high
from outside. For all, again, existing buildings, parish boundaries,
and denominational divisions can act as obstacles to genuine urban
outreach. Instead, what is needed is a focus upon people and
especially upon those outside existing churches.

If McGavran's three kinds of church growth are recalled –
biological, transfer, and conversion – then both he and the authors
of *Faith in the City* are most concerned about the third group. They
may not agree about the term 'conversion', but they do agree that at
present most of the energies and structures of urban churches are
suitable only for 'biological growth'. And in contemporary Britain
this leads to decline and to the by-passing of the greater part of the
urban population. To reach this population, churches will need to
start afresh by building up small, local worshipping communities.
Once established, McGavran believes that they in turn will need
church buildings. Yet ideally even these will not be supplied 'from
outside'.

Three broad processes of what sociologists term socialization
may be distinguished – processes through which we learn to
identify with particular systems of beliefs and associated patterns of
behaviour. The first of these is primary socialization. From birth we
are socialized into a system of beliefs and patterns of behaviour.
Our parents, our family, our school, our neighbours and our

immediate environment all contribute to this process. As we become more conscious of the outside world, so the network of our socialization may become further and further extended. As a result of this we may grow increasingly distant from our original beliefs and associated behaviour. The second process, which might be termed re-socialization, depicts the way we may eventually come back to our roots and identify once more with the system of beliefs and patterns of behaviour in which we were originally socialized. A third process, which might be termed trans-socialization, depicts the way we may change from one system of beliefs and patterns of behaviour to another. Viewed from the perspective of a single system of beliefs and patterns of behaviour, primary socialization is the process through which adherents are raised, re-socialization is the process through which they return to be adherents, and trans-socialization is the process through which those who have never previously been adherents become adherents.

If church membership is seen in terms of these three broad processes, it might lead to a fresh understanding of church strategy. Primary socialization refers to the process through which churches attempt to nurture 'biological' members. Sunday school, family eucharist, confirmation preparation, Bible study and discussion groups, and much of the preaching which takes place in church services is concerned with this process. Re-socialization refers to the process through which churches seek to rekindle Christian beliefs and practices in those who have grown distant from them. In the life-cycle of many there is likely to be a middle period, often commencing immediately before or immediately after confirmation (depending how early it is), when active church membership ceases. A key moment of personal change ('liminality' to use the technical term) – the birth of the first-born, the starting at school of a child, retirement, bereavement or serious illness – may prompt such an individual to return to active church membership. Trans-socialization refers to the process through which churches seek to draw into their membership those who have had little or no church primary socialization. Whereas few in modern Britain will be entirely ignorant of Christianity, an increasing section of the population has had little or no primary socialization in the churches.

These three processes require quite distinct strategies. Primary socialization is the process which is most familiar to churches. It involves the patterns of worship and nurture that are most in evidence in urban churches. As churches decline it may even become the only pattern of socialization that most churches offer. For example, it is significant that the family eucharist has become the central service in many Anglican churches (including my own). This service certainly does not exclude those who are not church members. Many Anglican churches today, following the pattern already well established amongst many Free Churches and within the Church of Scotland, have an 'open table' policy – inviting members of other denominations to share the sacrament. And many clergy today are more careful than was customary in the past to give out page references and brief explanations during a family eucharist. Yet it is clearly a form of service which favours those who are members and marginalizes those who are not. Again, the increasing reluctance of some clergy to baptize the children of nominal members or to marry nominal members, may be evidence of a shift towards primary socialization alone. Life-cycle rituals, which were once offered to all, become restricted to those who still adhere to their primary socialization.

If urban churches were seriously concerned with re-socialization, they might give more attention to a number of strategies. For example, they should be aware of the loss of membership associated with physical mobility. It will be remembered that this is the phenomenon whereby even key office bearers in one congregation may move to a new area and cease to go to church altogether. As clergy we are generally poor at referring to the clergy of their new parish members who move. Yet this is an obvious strategy. Further, most churches are poor at organizing their members systematically to invite new neighbours to their services. In this respect the Church of Scotland's lay eldership is, at its best, unusually well organized. The Church of England, in contrast, seldom has a system of elders or area wardens. All too often the congregation simply expects 'the vicar to do the visiting'. Indeed, in attempting to set up such a system the initial response of the church council was to imagine that I was asking them to compete with the Jehovah's Witnesses. Nothing so blatant is necessary, or even effective (Jehovah's Witnesses really do not 'convert' very many).[22] If the focus is upon re-socialization, not trans-socialization, there may be a very limited objective of encouraging the newly arrived to come to church or of locating others in need of pastoral support.

Again, churches which were sensitive to re-socialization might give more attention to the crucial moments of change/liminality that individuals face. For years the town clergy in my deanery discussed the need 'to do something' in a growing housing estate. It already contains perhaps forty per cent of the total population of the deanery and yet has no church building and its occupants play little role in the local churches. It was finally a conservative evangelical group that founded a house-church there and started family services in a local school. The group that they attracted particularly to these services were young mothers and their children. The group recognized more clearly than the professional clergy that a crucial moment of change (having children) can be a time for re-socialization or even trans-socialization. In many urban areas even bereavement and illness are not moments for parochial pastoral contact. Clergy 'do duty' at crematoria and effectively eliminate any possibility of continued pastoral contact with the bereaved. Hospital chaplains minister (often with great professionalism) to the ill, but again without any prospect of sustained pastoral contact once people leave hospital. In other words, key moments when re-socialization is possible are missed by local churches. An opportunity to welcome former church members back into a worshipping community is passed over.

However, it is trans-socialization which is most misunderstood by churches and for which they least have effective strategies. I have argued throughout this book that conservative evangelicals often misunderstand the nature of modern Britain. They tend to presume that those outside the churches need only to hear a simplistic account of the gospel to be 'converted'. Clear biblical witness is all that is required to bring the people back to the churches. Evangelical rallies and crusades can change 'pagan' Britain and turn it back into a Christian country. In the United States the so-called Tele Evangelists tell their people similar things. Claiming enormous (but probably spurious)[23] television audiences, they have claimed to represent Middle America and even sought much of the credit for Reagan's election. Not only do these conservative evangelicals misunderstand the nature of an increasingly educated and pluralist society, but they also confuse re-socialization with trans-socialization. Those who have already been socialized into churches (and perhaps have temporarily lapsed) form their primary audience. There is little evidence to suggest that they are particularly effective at trans-socialization. Indeed, anyone who listens to them with any care will soon realize that their preaching, and especially their appeals to biblical authority, *presuppose conservative Christian beliefs in their hearers.*

If urban churches are to edge beyond decline in Britain, they will need to devise new strategies for trans-socialization. In many areas energetic and enthusiastic clergy will need to start afresh. They will need to begin from the local community and work upwards. And to do this several factors are particularly crucial.

The first of these is deployment. If the Church of England really means business, it will plough its considerable resources into deploying stipendiary clergy, not into the countryside, but into areas of urban need. It may even be possible for the more privileged urban parishes to encourage some of their own members to consider a non-stipendiary ministry in a UPA. As yet non-stipendiary ministry is not always used very effectively. After three years of hard training, non-stipendiary clergy can sometimes find that they become little more than occasional preachers and visitors in relatively privileged urban parishes. Not surprisingly, tensions are regularly reported between non-stipendiary and stipendiary clergy[24] – especially when the latter arrive fresh in a parish to find a non-stipendiary priest who has effectively been in charge of the parish during the interregnum. If, instead, non-stipendiary clergy were given more independent roles, then some might be encouraged to take on a rural charge, whilst others might experiment with new forms of ministry in UPAs. Yet none of this should detract from the need for churches to use their financial resources to deploy as many stipendiary clergy into UPAs as possible. A good test of the seriousness of churches might well be to see how much of their resources they really are prepared to devote to UPAs.

A good test for many stipendiary clergy might also be for them to ask a number of key questions. To those clergy who have read up to this point: Does your parish raise the full cost of your stipend, housing and pension? If it does not, from where do the extra finances come? If they come from central funds, could they be better used in a situation of greater need? If they could, should you not be pressing your church for change?

Secondly there are buildings. By-passing existing structures, clergy deployed in UPAs will 'plant churches', develop 'small neighbourhood-based worship centres', 'base communities', 'worshipping communities', or whatever one chooses to call them.

The stress will be on the local and the community-based, not upon the public crusade. It may also become evident that existing church buildings actually contribute to church decline. The most obvious reason for this is that UPAs, especially the large council estates that have grown up on the edges of many cities, are often without church buildings. Populations have shifted and church buildings have been left stranded. The less obvious reason is that existing urban church buildings can easily become a full-time job in their own right.

McGavran's work, it will be recalled, started with the observation that in the Third World the 'mission station' was a hive of activity, as a self-contained entity, which actually had little impact on society at large. Those who have observed mission stations at first-hand will be aware that they tend to generate a full-time and exhausting routine which may have little to do with the outside community. I have observed missionaries working exceedingly hard, acting as hosts to visiting church dignitaries (ironically often from sponsoring churches or missionary agencies), supervising the station, operating the radio telephone, organizing transport, and doing a hundred other such tasks, few of which involved any outreach or social action in the wider community. Similarly, I have observed hard-pressed urban colleagues in Britain, and often their spouses too, inundated with telephone calls, visitors at the door, requests to supervise church building maintenance, and again a hundred other similar tasks revolving around church structures. The paradigm for the Victorian urban church was a whole cluster of buildings – a large church, church hall, vicarage, curate's flat, school – to be run by a small army of people. In depleted circumstances just the day-to-day running of this complex can soon become a full-time task for the single-handed clergyman. And then the buildings cease to be the tools for effective ministry for which they were designed. Rather they themselves become the central object of ministry.

If the new UPA clergy are to avoid this trap, they may need to start again without buildings and focus instead upon people. Weekly worship can be held in many other locations, as the house-church movement has shown. Without sharing its characteristic fundamentalism, mainline churches could be more courageous in emulating some of its practices. Schools or halls can be hired as needed. If buildings are eventually desired by the local community, then ideally they should be built, and then protected, by the local community.

Thirdly there is worship. The worship required in these settings must be sensitive to the culture dominant in the area. An Alternative Service Book with 1292 pages may not be the most suitable instrument for worship in a predominantly working-class neighbourhood. For those whose reading is habitually tabloid newspapers a book of any size may appear as an obstacle. In an age of visual aids and overhead projectors other means may be more suitable. Further, rites of passage will not be regarded as a chore by UPA clergy, but as a major opportunity to invite the population at large to worship. Folk religion and family services will be the staple diet of worship, rather than the eucharist. The latter is not an obvious means of trans-socialization.

Fourthly there is life-style. The clergy will live, not in middle-class isolation in a working-class area, but in council houses like their immediate parishioners. And, like them, their children may have to 'risk' going to local schools. In the Church of Scotland, quite disastrously, some UPA ministers live in manses comfortably placed outside their parishes *and* send their children to private schools. Total identity with the urban deprived is seldom possible. If nothing else, UPA clergy, unlike their parishioners, can always leave. Frequently, existing church buildings impose a middle-class identity upon individual clergy which they feel relatively powerless to overcome. Anyone who has lived in a spacious clergy house surrounded by terraced housing will at once be aware of this problem of imposed identity. In a number of UPAs the vicarage appears so socially isolated that it has become *the* house to burgle. Some real degree of local identification is essential if UPA clergy are to become more effective.

Yet herein lies a major problem which *Faith in the City* has correctly highlighted. UPA clergy can soon feel isolated from their colleagues and from the church at large. In this respect they can resemble rather closely those in an isolated rural ministry. There is nothing particularly new about clerical isolation and depression. Anyone who reads the endlessly fascinating Diary of Parson James Woodforde[25] can observe the same phenomenon, albeit in the late eighteenth century. In the last few years of his ministry in Norfolk, his apparent anxiety state was such that he felt unable, despite continuing personal piety, even to attend church. Like Parson

Woodforde, UPA clergy can soon find themselves surrounded by parishioners but not friends. This can even lead to a kind of autism in which effective action becomes increasingly difficult. Further the pressure caused by living in a community which responds only with difficulty to attempts to develop a worshipping community can exacerbate this clerical autism.

In this situation peer contact is essential. As an urban curate I was constantly grateful for being part of a large team. Regular contact with peers is important at several levels. It is important for humility. Isolated clergy, like isolated GPs, can soon take themselves too seriously. The dependent behaviour of many congregations towards their ministers helps to encourage this. Colleagues can tease and banter in ways not usually open to others. Peer contact is important for theological stimulation. Like many academics I am amazed when parish clergy confess, or even boast, to me that they 'never read theology'. I am often very tempted to ask them how they would feel if their GPs similarly claimed that they 'never read any modern medicine'. It would be unthinkable for most of my academic colleagues to ignore for long important books, whether directly in their field or not, when they are daily surrounded by the rest of us discussing them. Peer contact is also important for simple friendship. Because team or group ministries are still the exception they tend to be regarded with suspicion by many clergy and parishes. On several occasions I have seen just how difficult it is to overcome this suspicion. In country areas it can sometimes be considerably increased by teams being used as a means of amalgamating an ever increasingly number of small parishes. As a result teams and groups have a reputation for bickering and tension. If the life-style of UPA clergy in future is to include co-operation with peers as well as local indentification many will need to change very considerably. Clerical isolation – from both peers and the local community – may be yet another factor contributing to church decline.

Finally there are parish boundaries. *Faith in the City* stresses that mediaeval parish boundaries must be changed if UPAs are to have an effective ministry. Within many rural areas parish boundaries can still have some relationship to actual communities, although increasing rural amalgamation may sometimes work against them. In contrast, the five patterns of rural ministry that I have suggested seek to return to something like one priest per parish. However, in many UPAs parish boundaries make very little sense: effective boundaries here are much more likely to be ethnic, cultural and the product of social stratification. Curiously there is a tendency for declining churches actually to reinforce parish boundaries even in UPAs in which they are largely irrelevant. This tendency results from differing policies, particularly on baptism and church weddings, from one parish to the next. Whilst nominal adherents still seek these offices they soon discover that one parish responds to decline by restricting them to churchgoers and the next maintains an unrestrictive policy. Tension between the two parishes often emerges and the restrictive parish seeks to reinforce parish boundaries. This tension can even cross denominations. In part there is an irreconcilable theological difference involved here. But in part there is also an anachronistic geographical mentality.

For a national church the prospect of abandoning parish boundaries in UPAs is amongst the more radical suggestions of *Faith in the City*. Even in urban situations in which churches effectively have little more than a congregational role there is a strong reluctance to do this. Parishes define responsibilities and help to focus congregations on the community at large. Gathered congregations, in contrast, have a primary concern for their own members and can sometimes be quite distinct from the rest of society. They are more akin to clubs than to public institutions. A paradox emerges once more. The more effective a worshipping community becomes in an urban situation, the less it corresponds to the pluralism of this situation. It becomes one community amongst a number of differing communities. In contrast to the rural church, it can no longer be seen as the worshipping community of the community at large.

Within this situation I believe that a double perspective is required. It is important for national churches to think geographically at a central level. Indeed much of my criticism in this chapter has been that they do not do this with sufficient rigour. They fail to see the way existing rural deployment contributes to both rural and urban decline. However, at a local level UPAs require a perspective on natural communities rather than on inflexible geographic areas. If urban clergy could learn to co-operate more fully amongst themselves, they might learn that they have differing gifts to meet the needs of differing natural communities. They might also learn that the attempt to impose particular baptism or wedding policies upon whole areas will inevitably appear arbitrary to a population that does not itself think in parochial terms.

Once the focus in UPAs is upon natural communities, a more serious role than at present may be seen for the growing numbers of non-stipendiary clergy, particularly within London. If their employment does not allow them the flexibility of commuting or working from a rural base, it is vital that they should be offered real responsibility within an urban setting. Naturally this challenges existing structures. It is not easy for long-established stipendiary clergy to accommodate to the challenge of energetic non-stipendiary colleagues. And it is not always easy for those in authority to accept the loss of control that accompanies a voluntary work-force. The problems associated with urban non-stipendiary ministry lie more with existing structures than with the training, quality or enthusiasm of the non-stipendiary clergy themselves. Existing structures simply do not offer them sufficient pastoral responsibility. As a result, a great deal of talent and energy is under-used by urban churches and non-stipendiary clergy are inclined to feel disillusioned and unwanted.

If natural communities, rather than existing structures or parish boundaries, are the focus of ministry, non-stipendiary clergy can be challenged to minister to the communities most appropriate to their various gifts. Such clergy are only united by their lack of a parochial stipend. In every other respect they are as diverse as stipendiary clergy; some having teaching gifts, some pastoral gifts, some gifts with the young, some with the handicapped, some with the old, and many other gifts beyond. A ministry (whether stipendiary or non-stipendiary) which focusses upon natural communities does not expect individuals to have all of these gifts. Quite oppositely, it expects them to make the fullest use possible of the specific gifts that they are fortunate to possess.

Ministry organized in terms of natural communities will need co-ordination. And this may indeed be a function – a very demanding function – for the stipendiary clergy. However, co-ordination should not be confused with control. It is vital that those with specific responsibilities themselves have this control. Without this, non-stipendiary clergy would soon return to their predominant present role as perpetual assistant curates. Churches must learn to trust the urban non-stipendiary clergy that they have encouraged to be ordained. An effective team involves a mixture of individual autonomy and responsibility, mutual trust and co-operation, and overall co-ordination. Perhaps it is only finally in such a team that a really effective use of stipendiary and non-stipendiary clergy is possible in an urban setting. The critical needs of UPAs may make effective teams a prerequisite.

At the heart of my structural proposals for both rural and urban churches is a theological commitment. It is that active worshipping communities provide a central focus for churches and their ministry. This theological basis has become increasingly evident in recent critical understandings of ministry. If once it could be assumed by denominational theologians working separately that their particular form of ordained ministry was the one sanctioned by the New Testament, a more critical and ecumenical theology has suggested otherwise.[26] Whether the claims are about the threefold ministry, democratic presbyterianism, or the Petrine basis of the papacy, there is now a growing critical recognition that there is not just a single, fixed pattern of ministry present in the various writings of the New Testament. Rather there are various ways of serving worshipping communities. 'Orders' do not exist independently of these communities.[27] Ministry is rather primarily about service within specific communities.

One of the saddest features of the current debate within the Church of England about the ordination of women is that it has returned to denominational theology. Too often within the debate it is assumed that the New Testament does offer both a single, fixed pattern of ministry and even a concept of 'ordination' to a priesthood existing independently of specific worshipping communities. If ministry is seen instead as service to such communities, it is difficult to imagine that the polemic against the ordination of women could be sustained with any theological credibility.

A vision of ministry as service to specific worshipping communities has profound implications for both rural and urban situations. The ways of providing a largely unpaid rural ministry that I have suggested assume that ministry for *all* clergy is made meaningful in terms of active service to a specific community. That has indeed been my own experience and I am convinced that it could be the experience of others – non-stipendiaries, diocesan clergy, and the active recently retired. My suggestions for urban ministry assume that it is natural communities and not buildings or even geographic areas which should provide the primary focus. The priority in terms of resources that should be given to urban populations stems from a recognition that much greater flexibility and energy is needed if worshipping communities are to be maintained and developed in this more difficult situation. A more serious commitment to urban Britain is essential if churches really are to edge beyond decline.

And will churches have the vision and courage to make these changes? Well, they could. Or will they persist with existing structures and continue to decline? I am afraid that they might. They will need vision if they are to see the consequences of their current structures, and they will need courage if they are to effect a new vision. But it has been done before. The British churches in the middle of the last century did have vision and courage and did effect new structures. Unfortunately churches today have been slow to recognize that their structures should not be our structures. The rural parish with its own full-time, stipendiary clergyman and the urban parish with its array of church related buildings served their function once. Today they have become an encumbrance promoting not renewal but decline. It is time to change.

6

Faith Beyond Decline

Structures are important – but only as means not as ends. Our end as Christians is our relationship to God in Christ. It is important to specify the structures that best serve this end in each age and culture afresh, yet it is also vital that the structures do not become ends in themselves. The final temptation of declining churches is to imagine that, once the most effective structures have been found, all will be well. In contrast I wish to finish this book as a theologian rather than as a sociologist. Faith – understood as our relationship to God in Christ – should be at the very centre of our concern for churches as they seek to edge beyond decline.

In his trenchant style Bryan Wilson depicted the way clergy in the mid-1960s responded to decline (their own decline in social status and the numerical decline of the churches to which they belonged):

> Some obviously see social work and welfare as their appropriate role, from work with youth groups to organizations like the Samaritans. Others see themselves as responsible for social protest against the political structure of society, and enlist themselves into movements like CND and Anti-Apartheid, substituting for traditional hymnology the music of protest ... Others emphasize pastoral work in their communities and attempt to salve the abrasions which man living in highly institutionalized society is likely to suffer. Still others turn to ritual, as the irreducible religious function, capable of extension and elaboration, and the real professional expertise of the priest ... All of these are the new responses, the defence mechanisms, mounted for professional survival. Not least important, there is the ecumenical movement.[1]

In *Religion in Secular Society* Wilson argued at length that the rationalism and increasing bureaucracy which typify modern secular society play an ever-growing role in declining churches. Both the clergy and the churches as institutions respond to decline by adopting secular means which ironically contribute further to their own decline. It was in the ecumenical movement that he saw this as most evident. Far from it being a movement which depended ultimately upon theology, he saw theology as one of the early victims of the movement. For example, he suggested that when 'several denominations maintain large premises close together, duplicate administration, services, printing houses, missionary endeavour, fund-raising, prayer meetings – and each, often, with surplus capacity in terms of seating, and other facilities – then it becomes increasingly apparent, to men used to the rational economic thinking of the modern world that resources are under-used'.[2]

This he believed led to an increasing pressure towards ecumenism. It was, though, a pressure which subordinated theology to bureaucracy. In this, 'the new administrators of the Church, sometimes trained in the methods of modern business as much as in the theology of their denomination, begin increasingly to see possibilities for organizational change the only hindrances to which are the particular differences in belief and religious practice between denominations. The specific ideals for which denominations arose are then surrendered for the more rational use of resources, and for the greater convenience of administration.'[3]

Most churchpeople today might see this as a caricature. It soon became clear in the late 1960s that theological differences were capable of preventing church amalgamations,[4] however desirable they might have seemed in bureaucratic terms. Further the dramatic way that theological faculties in Britain have become genuinely ecumenical over the last twenty years may owe little to the social pressures suggested by Wilson. For most of us who teach in them, they result rather from a liberation from exclusive denominational theology and a recognition that critical scholarship crisscrosses existing ecclesiastical boundaries.

Yet, having argued that, there is a response to church decline which appears to turn inwards upon church structures and away from society at large. Even if he was wrong to see the whole of the ecumenical movement in these terms, Wilson may have been correct in a part of his analysis. In a passage that could equally be applied to those who focus exclusively upon church structures and deployment, he argued:

> What must be recognized, however interesting as the ecumenical movement may be, is that ecumenicalism, even at its most successful, is not in itself a revival of religion, nor a reconversion of society. It is the turning in on itself of institutionalized religion, as its hold on the wider social order has diminished. The healing of divisions is something which restores the morale of churchmen – and in a secular society a larger proportion of churchmen are professional churchmen – in a period when the external influence of the Church is declining either in terms of numbers of Church supporters in the wider population, as in England, or in terms of Christian influence over behaviour and morality, politics, education and other institutions as in the United States. The energy which churchmen have put into the ecumenical movement has been perhaps in rough proportion as they have lost hope of evangelization of the world. Essentially this has been a movement directed inwards into the life of the Church, not outwards into the wider society, which remains essentially unmoved by ecumenical achievement, and perhaps even rather suspicious of it.[5]

Despite my own practical and theological commitment to ecumenism, I believe that ecumenism as an institutional process can become a symptom of decline. Wilson may even be accurate when he cites the evidence to the effect that 'ecumenism may be a policy not only induced by decline, but one encouraging decline'.[6] Ecumenism seen as the amalgamation of church structures may actually contribute to numerical decline[7] as effectively as does the amalgamation of rural parishes. Further, an increasing amount of time and energy is spent by senior clergy in many churches in interchurch dialogue and conferences. Although at one level dialogue is essential for greater understanding, it can soon become an end in itself. Ecumenism is only a process. Our common relationship to God in Christ is the foundation and the end.

If inter-church dialogue is given too high a profile it may promote several distortions. One has already been noted in the first chapter. It tends to foster the presumption that individual churches do have, or at least ought to have, unified patterns of beliefs which can be mutually compared. In the process, a level of doctrinal uniformity is assumed which bears little relationship to the empirical reality of present-day Christianity.

In a trenchant critique of the 1982 *Final Report* of the Anglican-Roman Catholic International Commission (ARCIC), Paul Avis argues a very similar position. He is fully aware of the ecumenical importance of the report and of its eirenic intentions. Yet he is also aware that it tends to overlook the doctrinal pluralism that is becoming an ever more evident feature of Roman Catholic critical theology. The report presumes uniformity when it is in reality pluralism that increasingly represents Roman Catholic, as well as Anglican, theology. Avis prefaces his book with a, perhaps surprising, quotation from John Henry Newman: 'You cannot have Christianity and not have differences.' He points to the doctrinal pluralism that was recognized by Karl Rahner in 'Pluralism in Theology and the Unity of the Creed in the Church'[8] and regards Yves Congar's recent *Diversity and Communion*[9] as highly significant. For Avis:

> Rahner's words are a despairing reflection on the ferment within contemporary Roman Catholicism world-wide. The problem that he describes could only become exacerbated (if that was possible) in a united Church into which other traditions – each containing their own diversity – had been incorporated. Yet this whole dimension of pluralism within the churches is ignored by the ARCIC statement, though the fact of pluralism undermines the assumption of the report that it is possible for the Church to come to a common mind and feasible for its teaching authority to make decisions that are both relevant to the situation and universally binding, let alone free of error.[10]

Avis adds to his book *Ecumenical Theology* the subtitle *and the Elusiveness of Doctrine*. This gives an important clue to the alternative view of ecumenism that he offers. In manner close to my own argument, he concludes that his contentions about pluralism, 'on the face of it so disconcerting, in fact contain the seeds of hope for an approach to Christian unity that respects both the transcendent mystery of God and the personal nature of religious affirmations'.[11]

Secondly inter-church dialogue may actually impede the ability of individual churches to make changes to meet the needs of society at large. The issue of the ordination of women in the Church of

England is again a very obvious example of this. Teaching both male and female ordinands at Edinburgh, I am quite convinced that both are called by Christ and that both have gifts to offer a society which is increasingly learning to appreciate the role of women in the work place. Yet the well-publicized warnings of Cardinal Hume about the damage that the ordination of women might do to ecumenism have over-ridden such considerations for some. And this is despite the obvious points; that women are already ordained as priests in several parts of the Anglican Communion; that the dominant celibacy of Roman Catholic priesthood remains an impediment for most Anglican clergy; and that feminists within the Roman Catholic Church are themselves pressing for ordination.

Thirdly it promotes the view that the primary focus of ecumenism should be dialogue rather than practice. The reality of the situation is quite the reverse. Whilst church leaders and church theologians discuss the issue of the validity of orders, clergy across churches mutually recognize each others' orders in their very actions together. Even clerical colleagues who insist to me that episcopal ordination is essential for the validity of orders, *in practice* treat neighbouring Methodist and Church of Scotland ministers as fellow clergy. Further, whilst there is still theoretical argument about whether inter-communion should come before or after unity, Christians up and down the country are already taking part in each others' communion services. And whilst ecumenical discussions agonize over the ordination of women, women themselves are already beginning to assume a near-priestly role even within the Church of England. As Congar points out, inter-church agreements are 'the agreements of theologians ... acceptance by the grass roots is yet another question'.[12]

In contrast, I am increasingly convinced that ecumenism is primarily about practice and that theory will have to catch up with practice. In terms of praxis theology, inter-church theory which is so painfully at odds with current practice is quite simply inadequate. Even as a theologian, I find that ecumenism has more to do with my particular congregation sharing our church building every Sunday with the local Roman Catholics and learning to work, pray and study together with the Church of Scotland congregation, than it has to do with ARCIC or with other similar inter-church dialogues. As a result of the ecumenical movement, local worshipping communities can now be much more meaningful expressions of our common relationship to God in Christ. Sharing communion with my colleagues at work, or sharing activities with local Roman Catholics or Presbyterians in the Borders, does indeed for me express this common relationship. None of us really has to wait for any commission to tell us whether or not a particular church's orders or practices are valid.

Once faith is seen as our common relationship to God in Christ, several misunderstandings are removed. It would be foolish to imagine that any particular church could have a monopoly of truth about this relationship. It would be foolish to imagine that any creed, set of dogmas or doctrines, or indeed words of any kind, could capture this relationship. It would even be foolish to imagine that the written pages of the Bible can wholly capture this relationship.

Again, the veteran ecumenist and Dominican, Yves Congar, summarizes this perception of ecumenism in a manner which strips away ecclesiastical pretensions:

> No church or communion has succeeded in convincing the rest that it is in possession of *the* truth. Despite the profundity of its tradition and its constant affirmation that it is the solution of all our problems, the Orthodox church has not succeeded in convincing the rest of us that we must return to its fold. Nor has the Catholic church, despite its wealth of arguments, succeeded in convincing others of its papal dogma. Despite their learning and the vitality of their faith in Jesus Christ as saviour, the Protestants have not convinced others that they *are* the *Reformed* church. Nor has the Anglican communion, despite its concern to unite Reformed and traditional Catholicism, effectively been the bridge church which it claims to be.[13]

If our intimate relationships with each other go beyond our verbal expressions of them, then how much more will our relationship to God. It is characteristic of lovers to express their relationship with each other through analogy, through poetry, or perhaps most often through baby-talk. It was characteristic of the Jesus who appears in the Synoptic Gospels to express human relationships to God through parables, through images and even through the baby-talk of 'Abba'. Interpersonal relationships are literally irreducible: the signs that we use to express them are not the relationships themselves and can never adequately express them. They are at best approximations or signals to others which they will never understand unless they refer directly to their own finite relationships. How much more will this be true of our relationship to God who is infinite.

We use words to express relationships because otherwise we would be unable to express and interpret our relationships to each other. Yet, if we are thoughtful, we are careful not to confuse a relationship with words or to reduce it to words. Words can certainly reinforce relationships and, of course, they can also help to destroy them. Words are not a matter of indifference. Indeed most religions pay a great deal of attention to the words that they use to depict transcendence, regarding some words as more suitable than others. Even sounds may acquire particular significance in some traditions. However, across religious traditions, key theologians have insisted that finite language can only point to, rather than describe, that which is infinite.

In a remarkably bold recent book, Keith Ward examines a number of key thinkers from Hindu, Buddist, Jewish, Christian and Muslim traditions. He argues that 'there is a convergence of thought among at least the most reflective theologians or philosophers'.[14] This convergence is less apparent in the actual words that they use to express 'eternity', which are at best always unsatisfactory, than in a common pattern. This pattern is based upon a common vision of someone or something as the 'icon' or manifestation of eternity. It leads to a new self-understanding and to the conviction that one's true self is in that Self. And it produces submission and lifelong, all-demanding self-discipline.

Amongst the theistic traditions of Judaism, Christianity and Islam, this relationship is naturally expressed in personal terms. God is seen in terms of 'love', 'care', 'justice', etc. Yet it is axiomatic to philosophers working within these traditions that such human terms apply to God analogically or by extension. Indeed, it is frequently pointed out that the word 'holy' is most unusual in that its primary reference is to God: it applies analogically to humans. Most of the attributes applied to God – the lover, the carer, the judge, the shepherd, etc. – are primarily human depictions applied analogically to God. As a result, the term 'holy' appears mysterious in its own right and joins a term such as 'sacred', or neologisms such as 'numinous' or 'charismatic', to refer to qualities which **transcend the mundane.**

Christianity inherits personalist theism from Judaism, but to this it adds the personalism of the incarnation. The God-language of all Christian traditions is inescapably bound up with the person of Christ. Christian worship is thoroughly christo-centric, as anyone will soon discover if they devise a Jewish-Christian service. Even Jewish psalms are frequently given Christian doxologies in worship and Christians can easily offend Jews by referring to the 'Old' Testament and especially by interpreting it in the light of the 'New' Testament. Most Christian prayers, hymns, calendars and images are christo-centric, whatever the tradition. Viewed from outside surely anyone would conclude that as Christians, despite all our many differences, we are remarkably christo-centric. And as a result Christians are inevitably personalist in their relationship to God.

Once this personalism is fully appreciated, the pluralism of the New Testament and subsequent Christianity is a natural corollary. Since personal relationships can never be captured irreducibly in words, it is only to be expected that the different writers of the New Testament will use differing and sometimes contradictory words and ideas to express their relationship to God in Christ. It is also to be expected that this pluralism will be increased by subsequent generations of Christians coming from radically different social contexts and cultures.

My own technical research on theology as a social system[15] starts from this crucial link between, on the one hand, Christian faith viewed as a relationship to God in Christ and, on the other, endlessly changing cultures attempting to express this relationship in finite and relative words. If the relationship between God and humans is permanent, then the words that humans use to express this relationship most certainly are not. Even biblically derived terms must be chosen in preference to other biblical terms, must be mediated through differing languages and thought-forms across centuries of changing use, and then must be appreciated by persons of varying intelligence and experience. If a relationship is primary, socially relative words and concepts can at best be regarded as mediators. As such these words and concepts are properly the concern of the sociology of knowledge. It is my contention that this discipline can help theologians to a new understanding of their own role and function. Viewed as a social system theology need not be **reduced to a purely relative enterprise – as long as it is viewed as an** attempt to articulate a relationship to God in Christ. It is this latter relationship which provides the continuum, not the relative and changing words that are used to express it. Words are essential, but nonetheless culturally specific and socially relative. It is the relationship which is permanent, even if it can never be exhaustively expressed in finite and fallible words. In the end faith is beyond words.

This understanding of faith has a point of contact with both conservative evangelicals and with the radical position of Don Cupitt. It also has a fundamental difference from both. All evangelicals stress that faith is about a living relationship to God in Christ (or however this relationship is expressed). They are, I believe, correctly suspicious of theists who support their faith solely through intellectual means and have little or no recourse to corporate worship or private prayer. Faith is seen in dynamic not in static terms and Hebraic personalism is usually preferred to Hellenic abstraction. Yet conservative evangelicals usually wish to add to this the claim that the written words of the Bible offer an infallible and exhaustive account of this relationship. What they seldom realize is that these two claims – faith viewed as a relationship and the Bible viewed as infallible – actually pull in opposite directions. Dynamic relationships from their very nature cannot be captured in written words.

It is more curious still that Anglican conservative evangelicals who so strongly attacked the Bishop of Durham also insisted that the Creeds, and even the 39 Articles, must be believed literally. Not only does this insistence sit uncomfortably with a dynamic, relational approach to faith, but it is also surprisingly unbiblical. Both the Creeds and the 39 Articles contain terms not be found in the Bible. Of course this will not necessarily be of concern to those who already reject the infallibility of the Bible. Yet it presumably should be of concern to conservative evangelicals.

In complete contrast, Don Cupitt has long been aware of the pluralism of Christian doctrines and of the social relativity of expressions of Christian faith. However, increasingly he has come to question the relationship which is fundamental to my own understanding of faith. The difference between our positions is instructive. Cupitt's perception of doctrinal pluralism and social relativity has increasing led him to reject the concept of transcendence[16] in a pluralistic and secular age. My own analysis works in the reverse direction. My observation of doctrinal pluralism and social relativity points me to the difficulties inherent in depicting a transcendent relationship *in any age*. For me doctrinal pluralism is evidence consistent with this relationship. For Cupitt, I suspect, it rather counts against this relationship. Or, perhaps more accurately, it has pointed him along a path which has eventually led him to reject it.

Fifteen years ago, in arguing against the critic Walter Kaufmann, he showed that he was well aware of doctrinal pluralism. He argued that Kaufmann's criticism of theology[17] (like those of many other critics) presumed a monolithic version of theology which did not exist in practice:

> Here is a difficulty in his position: for theologies have been more diverse, and diverse in more ways, than he allows. As an illustration of diversity of *content* among theologians whose 'orthodoxy' is generally accepted, one might contrast the treatment of Christ's incarnation, death, and Resurrection, by St Paul and St John, or by St Athanasius and St Anselm. As for diversity of *method*, it is clear that Schleiermacher, Calvin, and St Thomas Aquinas have quite different ideas as to what theology is and how you set about doing it. Again, some forms of Christianity have been relatively indifferent to theology.[18]

Over the last fifteen years there has been a much franker recognition of Christian pluralism amongst biblical theologians,[19] systematic theologians[20] and exponents of Christian ethics.[21] If denominational theologians in the past could simply ignore this pluralism, it has become more difficult to do so today in ecumenical faculties. In this important respect Cupitt was writing ahead of some others at the time. For him, Kaufmann's weakness was that he 'supposes that he can frame a proposition about the Resurrection of Jesus which is clear in meaning – that is, can mean only one thing – and to which every theologian who can properly be called a Christian must assent. His whole case against theology depends upon this supposition: and it is false. Right from the beginning Christianity has been more diverse than people think: there never was, and never could be, one and only one orthodox set of beliefs.'[22]

However, the next step in Cupitt's argument is instructive. It is in this that one can see emerging the path that has led him more recently to reject transcendence altogether. An observation of

Christian pluralism convinced him of the need to reduce this pluralism. So he argued:

> Churches are hoarders, very bad at pruning out and discarding obsolete elements: or they are perhaps like coral reefs which grow by gradual accretion. There are numerous time-honoured popular Christian beliefs which are almost certainly false, super-stitious, and harmful. Belief in evil spirits is one of them. Some of these beliefs have in addition played a large part in theology. The belief in the virginal conception of Jesus by Mary is an example. We may think this belief to be of mythological origin, we may suppose that its rise was associated with mistranslation into Greek of an Old Testament text such as Isaiah 7:14. But however the belief arose it has done great harm. It has suggested that Jesus was not an ordinary man, it has helped to poison people's feelings about the process of reproduction, and it has encouraged ugly and useless forms of asceticism. So the belief ought to be abandoned.[23]

Cupitt's position here lacked some internal consistency. On the one hand he used Christian pluralism to combat Kaufmann and insisted that 'there never was, and never could be, one and only one orthodox set of beliefs'. Yet, on the other hand, he clearly did wish to prune Christianity of at least some of its doctrinal pluralism. The increasingly reductionist path that he has trodden since has been more in line with the latter than with the former. Yet ironically it may be more appropriate for a society which is uniformly secular than for one which is itself pluralistic.

I have argued elsewhere[24] that the moral and social consequences of theological concepts *are* relevant to an assessment of their validity. But an understanding of faith, as a relationship which can never be captured in words, should make one cautious before deciding too precipitately that some doctrines are to be anathematized. If faith is finally beyond words, then we should be more cautious about insisting upon either conservative or reductionist forms of 'orthodoxies'. As a Western, middle-class Anglican I inevitably find considerable difficulties in appreciating the Hispanic immigrant Catholicism of North America. The high position that it accords[25] to evil spirits and to Mary and the relatively low position that it gives to Christ are quite alien to me. Nonetheless I would hesitate long before applying Cupitt's moral judgments to it. At the very least I would have to know much more about the faith of such Catholics – in the relational terms that Cupitt has now also come to abandon. And the very elusiveness of such knowledge would probably preclude me from making such judgments.

If conservative fundamentalism represents one temptation for declining churches, theological reductionism may well represent another. This reductionism tends to suppose that, if the Christian faith is to be commended to a secular world, it must be translated into purely secular terms. Paul van Buren's *The Secular Meaning of the Gospel*[26] in the mid-1960s was one of the boldest attempts to do this. At the heart of this enterprise is an important pastoral concern and a real desire to engage with the secular world. It may, though, contain an important misunderstanding of this world. I have already argued that there is a growing consensus amongst sociologists of religion that Western society is more pluralistic than secular.

Of course there are secularists within Western pluralistic society – especially within the academic world. Yet even they have tended to be sceptical of secular theology. Some, like Kaufmann, would prefer theology to be monolithic and unsophisticated, presenting a much clearer target to attack. However, others have not unreasonably questioned why anyone should actually become a Christian when they must permanently dissent from the predominant theism of fellow Christians. They would rather remain friendly sceptics. It may be easier to see why some who are already Christians become secular Christians, than it is to see why those who deny being Christians should themselves become secular Christians. As a result, secular Christianity, despite its aims, may be less a means of commending Christianity to a secular society, than a means for those who are already Christians to adjust to what they suppose to be a secular society.

However it is the differing theological responses to doctrinal pluralism, between my own position and that of theological reductionism, which are the most crucial. Reductionists tend to argue that if we cannot accept a particular doctrine then we should abandon it. Their reasons for such rejection vary fairly considerably. For some it is modern biblical exegesis which leads to this rejection; for others it is the moral or social consequences of the doctrines; for others again it is their incompatibility with what they take to be present-day plausibility structures; for still others it is their association with what they regard as unacceptable forms of piety or spirituality. All of these elements can be found in the quotation from Don Cupitt. Yet they are different from each other and they will be variously convincing or unconvincing to different Christians.

In reality *all* thinking Christians must make choices and make mental reservations about doctrines or understandings of doctrines that are claimed by some to be Christian. Precisely because Christianity is so pluralistic and varied, it is simply not possible for anyone to accept all the many and sometimes contradictory doctrinal claims that are made within it. Perhaps all long-established religions are accumulative traditions.[27] Certainly all long-established churches are accumulative. Internal consistency is not their most obvious property. Christian maturity may have much to do with learning to come to terms with this. And Christian wisdom may require individuals to realize that their particular choices and reservations are not the only ones that could have been made. Genuine ecumenism may well depend upon such wisdom.

Again, if faith is seen in relational terms, Christians have good grounds for this wisdom. Relationships are more important than anything else in life. Yet they are intangible, elusive and finally inexpressible. How much more our relationship to God in Christ. The various writings which form the New Testament contain a rich and diverse pool of resources from which to draw in our attempt to articulate this relationship. For some of us in one age, culture or society, one set of resources will prove particularly helpful or challenging. However, for others in a quite different age, culture or society, it may be a different set. The resources themselves are too varied for all of us to use them all of the time. Selection is essential. Modern biblical hermeneutics is an attempt to do just that. Yet hermeneutics change, and we change, and in any case our faith is finally inexpressible.

In contrast, theological reductionists wish to choose for us by decisive pruning. They are curiously confident about their own criteria for doing this. They presume to know the needs of a pluralistic society. And they may even presume on the plausibility structures of a future society. If nineteenth-century theological reductionists had been successful in their attempts to prune, it is interesting to speculate on the purely individualistic version of Christianity that would have been bequeathed to the twentieth century. Reductionisms themselves change from one age to another. And yet they remain confident about their present criteria.

If we select rather than prune, we leave to one side objects we cannot appreciate. Others may well select differently and appreciate those objects we left. Time will show. If we keep dipping into the pool we may learn to appreciate the objects differently ourselves. I am only too conscious that when I was an honours New Testament student one of the selected passages – Mark 13 – was fascinating but quite incredible to me. Then it raised the crucial christological question, 'Did Jesus make a historical error in predicting the end of the world?' Today it raises quite different questions for me and appears distinctly less incredible. Rapid nuclear proliferation has meant that images of eschatological fragility have new and uncomfortable resonances. And the injunctions at the end of the chapter assume a new urgency. Radical eschatology – one of the most dangerous and distrusted features of Christianity – tends to resurface in quite unexpected places. But of course it would be one of the first elements to be pruned by many reductionists.

I am even conscious that I have learned much from forms of Christianity which I have never been able to adopt for myself. For example, I found Metropolitan (of the Orthodox Syrian Church of South India) Geevarghese Mar Osthathios' *The Sin of Being Rich in a Poor World* both challenging and theologically stimulating. It is not just an impassioned plea for the poor: it is also a reasoned account of a theological basis for this plea. Coming from the Eastern Orthodox tradition this basis is thoroughly trinitarian. So much so that in arguing for a social model of the Trinity as a nuclear family of Father, Mother and Son, Osthathios believes that we are given a model of socialist living as human beings. With passion he argues that 'Christian theology demands that we take the side of the poor for the liberation of the poor and the rich as shown in Christ. Liberation and reconciliation are the aims we have to keep before us even in our political action as we know them to be God's purpose for the whole of humanity.' This much could have been written by many other liberation theologians. But then he adds his distinctive contribution from the Eastern Othodox tradition: 'If the Holy Trinity is our theological basis for a classless society and the Cross the means of achieving it, we will be ready for humiliation, sufferings and even atoning death.'[28]

I cannot pretend that I find it easy to envisage the Trinity as 'a classless society', as 'a nuclear family', or even as a society at all. Osthathios is fully aware of suspicions of tritheism and insists that *perichoresis* 'unites the three in one and shares the one in three'.[29] Yet his understanding of the Trinity is so social that he argues that 'the Trinity is to be emulated as far as we can, by the power of the Holy Spirit'.[30] For him a social understanding of the Trinity provides the justification and basis for a more just and equal society. I believe that it is possible, even for those who cannot themselves adopt a social model of the Trinity, to learn from this.

Within my own tradition it is more natural to ground the social basis of faith in the Synoptic concept of the kingdom of God or in St Paul's concept of the body of Christ. At first, faith viewed as a relationship to God in Christ might seem excessively individualistic. It might even seem to contradict the weight I gave in the previous chapter to worshipping communities. I have, though, talked about 'our' relationship to God in Christ and, in the ecumenical context, 'our common' relationship to God in Christ. Further, once this relationship is set in the context of the Synoptic or Pauline models it can be seen as more corporate than individualistic. Our relationship to God in Christ is part of the kingdom of God. In the Synoptics, we 'enter' the kingdom of God (literally 'God's rule' rather than a place) – a kingdom which is both present in the healing, power and person of Jesus' ministry within the community, and which is also future. In Paul, as Christians we are 'in Christ' and our future together lies 'in Christ': we are incorporated into his body.

In nineteenth and early twentieth-century liberal theology much attention was given to the individual's 'experience' of God. Although this generated considerable psychological and phenomenological interest in the subject, it has proved less congenial for late twentieth-century theology. By focussing on individual experience, it tended to deflect attention from the social implications of theology. A relational theology, in contrast, need not be committed to any particular theory of individual religious experience. It can encompass those who are convinced that such experience is possible as well as those who are more sceptical. Relationships can include both those which are experienced person-to-person and those that are known only at a distance. If the relationship of lovers typifies the first, the relationship between ruler and ruled can typify the second. Both are widely used analogically to denote God's relationship to humans.

Faith seen in relational terms has both a social location and social implications. The natural location for faith, understood as our relationship to God in Christ, is in worship. Within a worshipping community we identify, express, purify, give praise for, and are challenged by, this relationship. The rich, but also varied, resources, accumulated within the Christian tradition, fashion these communities and provide the social context for these essential activities. Here we learn to support others and be supported ourselves in our common relationship to God in Christ. Or, to use more sociological terms, here is the locus of our primary socialization as Christians. And from here we can go out to transform the world at large. The values we seek to embed into society at large and the moral praxis that is so distinctive a feature of present-day churches, are generated, sustained and reconstituted within these worshipping communities.

Even when we are aware of the inevitable frailty of these communities, the rich resources that they, sometimes quite unconsciously, contain can still challenge and transform. It is significant that, despite the racism, sexism and classism apparent in Christian communities, the very resources that they are heirs to, and carriers of, can still be used to challenge these evils. The rich resources of Christianity – like those perhaps of many long-established religious traditions – offer abundant challenges to the communities they spawn. It may even take centuries (as it did on the issue of slavery) for these communities to understand the implications of these resources. Yet so long as worshipping communities continue to bear these resources, they remain to challenge a new generation afresh.

And it *is* within worship that the challenge is most potent. Undoubtedly some who have ceased to worship continue to study biblical, devotional and theological literature. There are even those identifying themselves as quite secular who are nonetheless fine scholars of religion. But for most of us, it is worship that transforms Christian literature, symbols and rituals, from being just interesting objects, into resources that can direct, challenge and renew. It is their place in worship, rather than any inherent infallibility, that imbues them with especial significance for most Christians. Within **popular worship even the most tawdry Catholic statue, the most** unctious Protestant hymn, or the most puerile Orthodox icon, can assume a position of profound significance for the worshippers themselves.

The peculiarity and potency of worship may soon be forgotten by regular participants. However, the total outsider will at once be impressed by the peculiarity. The potency may take longer to appreciate. Worship can act as a powerful constraint – as every preacher will know. Sermons, which are given so central a place in many forms of worship and in the concerns of ministers themselves, are subject to deep constraints and stereotypes. Yet worship can also act as a powerful enabler. Individuals can express praise and jubilation, penitence and commitment, in ways that they might seldom feel able to do in the rest of life. They can, so Christians believe, be empowered by the Spirit and regenerated in the Body of Christ. However this is expressed, renewal within worship is a common thread running across Christian traditions.

And for many of us as Christians it is finally in the eucharist that we become most conscious of our relationship to God in Christ. In sharing in this most christo-centric form of worship, our common relationship to God in Christ becomes most evident. The eucharist goes beyond words. It involves ritual actions of both imitation and participation. Its meaning remains as oblique to us as it no doubt did to the earliest Christians. Like all effective symbols and rituals it is irreducible and *sui generis*. Even when élites within some Christian traditions have sought to impose a single, unambiguous interpretation of the eucharist, others have soon offered a contradictory alternative. Viewed as a central enactment of our common relationship to God in Christ, the eucharist inevitably defies such univocity.

In churches edging beyond decline the eucharist is central. It does not provide the obvious form of worship for those at present outside formal church structures. But for those who do attend regular worship it is already assuming an ever more central position. As we cross church boundaries and discover our varied, rich heritage of resources, we increasingly learn to share the eucharist together. Beyond decline we may learn tolerance of our differences of practice and interpretation. As we begin to glimpse faith as our common relationship to God in Christ, we may learn to distinguish our own necessary, but partial and finite, understandings from the relationship itself.[31] Then we will have glimpsed faith beyond the temptations of declining churches.

Notes

Introduction

1. CUP 1977.
2. Geoffrey Chapman and Paulist Press 1987.
3. See further, Robin Gill, 'Theology – a Social System: Models for a Systematic Theology', *Scottish Journal of Theology*, forthcoming.

1 Decline and the Gulf between Theory and Practice

1. See further my *Prophecy and Praxis*, Marshall, Morgan and Scott 1981. For a very full technical discussion see Rudolf J. Siebert, *The Critical Theory of Religion*, Mouton 1985.
2. E.g. in my *The Social Context of Theology*, Mowbrays 1975 and *Theology and Social Structure*, Mowbrays 1977.
3. Paul Badham in *The Expository Times*, 97.10, July 1986, p.294.
4. Cf. Alistair Kee, *Domination or Liberation*, SCM Press 1986: see also Bryan S. Turner, *Religion and Social Theory*, Heinemann 1983.
5. See Richard L. Gorsuch and Daniel Aleshire, 'Christian Faith and Prejudice: Review of Research', *Journal for the Scientific Study of Religion* 13, 3, 1974; and C. D. Batson and W. L. Ventis, *The Religious Experience*, OUP 1982.
6. See Clifford Hill, 'Some aspects of Race and Religion in Britain', *A Sociological Yearbook of Religion in Britain 3*, ed David Martin and Michael Hill, SCM Press 1970; John Fethney, article in *Race Today*, January 1973; and Donely T. Studlar, 'Religion and White Racial Attitudes in Britain', *Ethnic and Racial Studies* 1, 3, July 1978.
7. Badham, art. cit., p. 295.
8. See Rosemary Ruether, *Faith and Fratricide*, Seabury Press, NY 1974; Gregory Baum, *Religion and Alienation*, Paulist Press 1975; and Charlotte Klein, *Anti-Judaism in Christian Theology*, SPCK 1978.
9. E.g. N. J. Demerath, 'Religion and Social Class in America', *Sociology of Religion* ed Roland Robertson, Penguin 1969: but see, Kenneth

Thompson, 'Religion, Class and Control', *Religion and Ideology* ed Robert Bocock and Kenneth Thompson, Manchester University Press 1985.
10. Badham, art. cit., p. 295.
11. Ibid.
12. *The Nature of Christian Belief*, Church House Publishing 1986, para. 20.
13. Ibid., para. 12.
14. e.g. Keith Ward on Radio 4's programme *Sunday* immediately after publication.
15. *The Nature of Christian Belief*, para. 55.
16. Ibid., para. 44.
17. Ibid., para. 60.
18. Ibid., para. 61.

2   *The Gulf in Social Pronouncements*

1. See Edward Norman, *Christianity and the World Order*, OUP 1979. For a lively critique see Haddon Willmer (ed), *Christian Faith and Political Hopes*, Epworth Press 1979.
2. I cite the sociological literature on 'sects' in the next chapter.
3. For these, see further my *A Textbook of Christian Ethics*, T. & T. Clark 1985.
4. see Charles E. Curran (ed), *Absolutes in Moral Theology?*, Greenwood 1975, and *Issues in Sexual and Medical Ethics*, University of Notre Dame Press 1978; and James M. Gustafson, *Protestant and Roman Catholic Ethics*, University of Chicago Press and SCM Press 1978.
5. See Lane Committee, *Report of the Committee on the Working of the Abortion Act*, Vol. 3, HMSO 1974.
6. E.g. David Atkinson, *To Have and to Hold*, Collins 1979.
7. Church House Publishing 1987.
8. Ebehard Welty, *A Handbook of Christian Social Ethics*, 2 Vols, Nelson 1960–63.
9. E.g. Roger Ruston O P, *Nuclear Deterrence – Right or Wrong?* Catholic Information Service 1981.
10. National Council of Catholic Bishops, 1312 Massachusetts Avenue, N. W., Washington, DC, 3 May 1983 (re-printed CTS/SPCK 1983).
11. National Council of Catholic Bishops, as above, November 1986.
12. Andrew Greeley, *American Catholics Since the Council*, Thomas More Press 1985.
13. See my *The Cross Against the Bomb*, Epworth Press 1984.
14. See Anthony Archer, *The Two Catholic Churches*, SCM Press 1985.
15. Joseph Fitzpatrick, *One Church Many Cultures: The Challenge of Diversity*, Sheed and Ward 1987.
16. Ibid. p. 119.

17. Frank Gibson (ed), *Abortion in Debate*, Quorum Press, Church of Scotland 1987.

18. *Reports to the General Assembly*, Church of Scotland 1985, 3.2.

19. *Reports to the General Assembly*, Church of Scotland 1987, 3.1.

20. Ibid. 3.2.

21. *Abortion in Debate*, Quorum Press, Church of Scotland 1987.

22. Quorum Press, Church of Scotland 1987.

23. *Abortion in Debate*, p. 29.

24. See further my *Theology and Social Structure*, Mowbrays 1977.

25. *The Church and the Bomb*, Hodder and Stoughton 1982.

26. *The Cross and the Bomb*, Mowbrays 1983.

27. *The Cross Against the Bomb*, Epworth Press 1984.

28. Myron S. Augsburger and Dean C. Curry, *Nuclear Arms: Two Views on World Peace*, World Books, Waco 1987.

29. Ibid., p. 31.

30. Ibid., p. 68.

31. *The Cross and the Bomb*, p. 1.

32. See Roland H. Bainton, *Christian Attitudes Toward War and Peace*, Abingdon, Nashville 1960, and Hodder and Stoughton 1961.

3 *Social Action Beyond Decline*

1. An important exception is Mady Thung, *The Precarious Organisation*, Mouton 1976: see also her article in my *Theology and Sociology: a Reader*, Chapman 1987.

2. Macmillan 1979.

3. The classic approach is by Max Weber, *The Sociology of Religion* (1920), Beacon Press 1963, and Methuen 1965: see further my *Prophecy and Praxis*, Marshall, Morgan and Scott 1981.

4. See Harold E. Quinley, *The Prophetic Clergy*, John Wiley 1974.

5. See Leslie J. Francis, *Rural Anglicanism*, Collins 1985.

6. See Anthony Russell, *The Clerical Profession*, SPCK 1980: for the anthropological significance of 'masks' and uniforms, see F. G. Bailey's final chapter in *Gifts and Poison: The Politics of Reputation*, Blackwell 1971.

7. See S. Ranson, A. Bryman and B. Hinings, *Clergy, Ministers and Priests*, Routledge and Kegan Paul 1977.

8. See Josephine Butler, *Recollections of George Butler*, Bristol 1892, and *Personal Reminiscences of a Great Crusade*, London 1896.

9. See Ian Bradley, *The Call to Seriousness*, Jonathan Cape 1976.

10. See Michael Hill, *The Religious Order*, Heinemann 1973.

11. E.g. Weber, op. cit.

12. E.g. Rodney Stark and William Sims Bainbridge, *The Future of Religion*, University of California Press 1985.

13. E.g. Bryan Wilson, *Religion in Sociological Perspective*, OUP 1982; and Roy Wallis, *The Elementary Forms of the New Religious Life*, Routledge and Kegan Paul 1984.

14. See Roy Wallis, *The Road to Total Freedom*, Heinemann and Columbia University Press 1976.

15. See James A. Beckford, *The Trumpet Call of Prophecy*, Blackwell 1975.

16. See Christine King, 'The Case of the Third Reich', *New Religious Movements* ed Eileen Barker, Edwin Mellen 1982.

17. See Peter Brock, *Twentieth-Century Pacifism*, Van Nostrand Reinhold 1970.

18. See Bryan Wilson, *Religious Sects*, Weidenfeld and Nicolson 1970.

19. *The Kairos Document*, Braamfontein 1985.

20. Ibid., p. 3.

21. Ibid., p. 7.

22. Ibid., p. 8.

23. Ibid., p. 9.

24. Ibid., p. 12.

25. Ibid., pp. 13–14.

26. Ibid., p. 22.

27. Ibid., p. 1.

28. Ibid., p. 2.

29. See further my *Prophecy and Praxis*.

30. John Habgood, *Church and Nation in a Secular Age*, Darton Longman and Todd 1983, p. 1.

31. Ibid., p. 49.

32. Ibid., p. 37.

33. Ibid., p. 34.

34. Ibid., p. 40.

35. Ibid., p. 36.

36. Ibid., p. 43.

37. Ibid., pp. 168–9.

38. *Changing Britain: Social Diversity and Moral Unity*, Church House Publishing 1987, pp. 63f.

39. Ibid., p. 67.

40. See Duncan Forrester, *Theology and Politics*, Blackwell 1988: see also Sara Maitland's 'note of reservation' in *Changing Britain*, p. 70.

41. Cf. Duncan Forrester, *Christianity and the Future of Welfare*, Epworth Press 1985.

42. *Lifestyle Survey*, Quorum Press, Church of Scotland 1987, p. 192.

43. Ibid., p. 197.

44. Constable 1965.

45. See *Faith in the Scottish City*, Centre for Theology and Public Issues, University of Edinburgh 1986.

46. Eg. see Graham Melville-Thomas's review 'Television Violence and Children', *Video Violence and Children* ed Geoffrey Barlow and Alison Hill, Hodder and Stoughton 1985.

47. See further my *A Textbook of Christian Ethics*, T. & T. Clark 1985.

48. 10 January 1987.
49. 4 April 1987.
50. Vol. 80, May 1987, p. 283.

4 *Outreach Beyond Decline*

1. See Robert Currie, Alan Gilbert and Lee Horsley, *Churches and Churchgoers*, CUP 1977: and J. N. Wolfe and M. Pickford, *The Church of Scotland: An Economic Survey*, Chapman 1980, ch. 4.
2. See David Martin, *A General Theory of Secularization*, Blackwell 1978.
3. Eg. Bryan Wilson, *Religion in Secular Society*, Watts 1966, and *Contemporary Transformations of Religion*, OUP 1976.
4. Eg. Rodney Stark and William Sims Bainbridge, *The Future of Religion*, University of California Press 1985.
5. Eg. Thomas Luckmann, *The Invisible Religion*, Macmillan 1967.
6. For the arguments in this paragraph see Philip Hammond (ed), *The Sacred in a Secular Age*, University of California Press 1984.
7. Eg. David Martin, *The Religious and the Secular*, Routledge and Kegan Paul 1969.
8. Compare Wilson's initial article with the other articles in Philip Hammond (ed), *The Sacred in a Secular Age*.
9. Watts 1966.
10. OUP 1976.
11. See my *The Social Context of Theology*, Mowbrays 1975.
12. E.g. Bryan Wilson, *Religion in Sociological Perspective*, OUP 1982.
13. See John Habgood, *Church and Nation in a Secular Age*.
14. E.g. Bryan Wilson, *Religion in Secular Society*, Watts 1966.
15. See Victor Turner, *Image and Pilgrimage in Christian Culture*, Columbia 1978: an extract on liminality from this book appears in my *Theology and Sociology: a Reader*, Chapman 1987.
16. See Peter Brown, *Augustine of Hippo: a Biography*, University of California Press and Faber and Faber 1967.
17. See Barry Barnes, *Scientific Knowledge and Sociological Theory*, Routledge and Kegan Paul 1974. For a recent sociological discussion of the language of converts, see C. L. Staples and A. L. Mauss, 'Conversion or Commitment', *Journal for the Scientific Study of Religion*, 26, 2, June 1987.
18. Donald A. McGavran, *Understanding Church Growth*, Eerdmans 1980 (original edn 1970).
19. Ibid., p. 46.
20. Ibid., pp. 85–6.
21. Ibid., p. 418.
22. Ibid., p. 45.
23. Ibid., p. 48.

24. Ibid., p. 91.
25. Ibid., p. 93.
26. Ibid., p. 8.
27. Lesslie Newbigin, *The Open Secret*, SPCK and Eerdmans 1978, p. 140.
28. Ibid., p. 141.
29. Ibid.
30. McGavran, op. cit., p. 35.
31. Ibid., pp. 102–3.
32. Alistair Kee, *Domination or Liberation*, SCM Press 1986, p. 87.
33. Ibid., p. xi.
34. Ibid., p. xii.
35. Leonardo Boff, *Church, Charism and Power*, SCM Press and Crossroad Publishing Co. 1985.
36. Kee, op. cit., pp. 85–6.
37. Eg. Bryan Wilson, *Religion in Secular Society*, Watts 1966: for a critique of Wilson, and Berger's 'market analogy' of ecumenism, see Bryan S. Turner, 'The Sociological Explanation of Ecumenism', *The Social Sciences and the Churches* ed C. L. Mitton, T. & T. Clark 1972.
38. See A.P.D 'Entrèves, *Aquinas: Selected Political Writings*, Blackwell 1948.
39. *Faith in the City*, The Report of the Archbishop of Canterbury's Commission on Urban Priority Areas, Church House Publishing 1985, p. 3.
40. Ibid., p. 7.
41. McGavran, op. cit., pp. 98–9.
42. See Geoffrey K. Nelson and Rosemary A. Clews, *Mobility and Religious Commitment*, Institute for the Study of Worship and Religious Architecture, University of Birmingham 1971.

5 *Structures Beyond Decline*

1. See M. F. Wiles, *The Making of Christian Doctrine*, CUP 1967.
2. See Geoffrey Wainwright, *Doxology*, Epworth Press 1980.
3. See Stephen W. Sykes, *The Integrity of Anglicanism*, Mowbrays 1978: for a fuller treatment of 'identity' see his *The Identity of Christianity*, SPCK 1984.
4. Eg. David Martin, *The Breaking of the Image*, Blackwell 1980 and Richard K. Fenn, *Liturgies and Trials*, Blackwell 1982.
5. See Anthony Russell, *The Clerical Profession*, SPCK 1980 and *The Country Parish*, SPCK 1986.
6. Kenneth H. Vickers, *A History of Northumberland*, Vol. XI, Andrew Reid 1922, p. 100.
7. Leslie Paul, *The Deployment and Payment of the Clergy*, Church of England Information Office 1964.
8. See David Martin, *A General Theory of Secularization*, Blackwell 1978.

9. *Faith in the City*, Appendix B, Table 1.

10. Newcastle Diocesan Directory 1986.

11. Leslie J. Francis, *Rural Anglicanism*, Collins 1985, p. 93.

12. Ibid.

13. *Faith in the City*, p. 73.

14. Ibid., p. 74.

15. Eg. John Tiller, *A Strategy for the Church's Ministry*, CIO Publishing 1983.

16. See W. H. Saumarez Smith, *An Honorary Ministry*, ACCM Occasional Paper, No. 8, 1977: and Mark Hodge, *Non-Stipendiary Ministry in the Church of England*, CIO Publishing 1983.

17. *Faith in the City*, pp. 112f.

18. Francis, op. cit., p. 91.

19. Jacqueline Jolleys, 'Woman Physician: An Enviable Arrangement?', *The Physician* 6, 8, August 1987, p. 452.

20. *Faith in the City*, p. 90.

21. Ibid., p. 93.

22. See James A. Beckford, *The Trumpet Call of Prophecy*, Blackwell 1975.

23. See Jeffrey K. Hadden and Charles E. Swann, *Prime Time Preachers: The Rising Power of Televangelism*, Addison-Wesley 1981.

24. See Mark Hodge, op. cit.

25. OUP 1924 (paperback selection OUP 1978).

26. Eg. Bernard Cooke, *Ministry to Word and Sacraments*, Fortress Press 1976; and R. P. C. Hanson, *The Priesthood Examined*, Lutterworth Press 1979. See also James D. G. Dunn and James P. Mackey, *New Testament Theology in Dialogue*, SPCK 1987, chs 5 and 6.

27. See Edward Schillebeeckx, *Ministry*, SCM Press 1981, and *The Church with a Human Face*, SCM Press 1985.

6 *Faith Beyond Decline*

1. Bryan Wilson, *Religion in Secular Society*, Watts 1966, p. 85.

2. Ibid., p. 139.

3. Ibid., pp. 139–40.

4. See further, Robin Gill, 'British Theology as a Sociological Variable', *A Sociological Yearbook of Religion in Britain* 7, ed Michael Hill, SCM Press 1974.

5. Wilson, op. cit., pp. 175–6.

6. Ibid., p. 176.

7. Wilson points to the English evidence from Methodist amalgamations. Since he wrote, the United Reformed Church also suggests this. For similar empirical evidence from Presbyterian amalgamations in Scotland see J. N. Wolfe and M. Pickford, *The Church of Scotland: An Economic Survey*, Chapman 1980.

8. Karl Rahner, *Theological Investigations*, Vol. XI, Darton, Longman and Todd 1974.

9. Yves Congar, *Diversity and Communion*, SCM Press 1984.

10. Paul Avis, *Ecumenical Theology* SPCK 1986, p. 89.

11. Ibid., p. xv.

12. Congar, op. cit., pp. 140–1.

13. Ibid., p. 161.

14. Keith Ward, *Images of Eternity*, Darton, Longman and Todd 1987, p. viii.

15. See further, Robin Gill, 'Theology – a Social System: Models for a Systematic Theology', *Scottish Journal of Theology*, forthcoming.

16. See Don Cupitt, *Taking Leave of God*, SCM Press 1980; *The World to Come*, SCM Press 1982: *Only Human*, SCM Press 1984; *The Long-Legged Fly*, SCM Press 1987.

17. Ie. Walter Kaufmann, *The Faith of a Heretic*, Anchor 1963.

18. Don Cupitt, *Crisis of Moral Authority*, Lutterworth 1972; reissued SCM Press 1985, p. 151.

19. See James D.G. Dunn, *Unity and Diversity in the New Testament*, SCM Press 1977.

20. See Stephen W. Sykes, *The Identity of Christianity*, SPCK 1984 and Ruth Page, *Ambiguity and the Presence of God*, SCM Press 1985.

21. See James M. Gustafson, *Protestant and Roman Catholic Ethics*, University of Chicago Press and SCM Press 1978. Particularly relevant are recent sociological discussions of the differing ethical communities that constituted earliest Christianity; see Wayne A. Meeks, *The Moral World of the First Christians*, SPCK 1987 and Klaus Wengst, *Pax Romana and the Peace of Jesus Christ*, SCM Press 1987.

22. Cupitt, *Crisis of Moral Authority*, p. 153.

23. Ibid., pp. 154–5.

24. Ie. Robin Gill, *Prophecy and Praxis*, Marshall, Morgan and Scott, 1981.

25. See Joseph P. Fitzpatrick, *One Church Many Cultures: The Challenge of Diversity*, Sheed and Ward 1987.

26. SCM Press 1963.

27. See Wilfred Cantwell Smith, *The Meaning and End of Religion*, Macmillan 1963.

28. Geevarghese Mar Osthathios, *The Sin of Being Rich in a Poor World*, Christian Literature Society Madras 1983, pp. 63–4.

29. Ibid., p. 45.

30. Ibid., p. 52.

31. Cf. Ruth Page's conclusion to *Ambiguity and the Presence of God*: 'The only constant is God's continuing relationship with creation. Yet in and through and by means of Ambiguity, at every contingent place and time, among people of any age and culture, this relationship may be apprehended, God may be worshipped and all conceptions of the value and significance of experience transformed' (p. 216).

Index